THE

DAILY SPARK

180 easy-to-use lessons and class activities!

THE DAILY SPARK

Critical Thinking
Journal Writing
Poetry
Pre-Algebra
SAT: English Test Prep
Shakespeare
Spelling & Grammar
U.S. History
Vocabulary
Writing

THE

DAILY SPARK

SAT: English
Test Prep

SPARKNOTES is a registered trademark of SparkNotes LLC.

Spark Publishing
A Division of Barnes & Noble Publishing
120 Fifth Avenue
New York, NY 10011
www.sparknotes.com

ISBN-13: 978-1-4114-0223-2
ISBN-10: 1-4114-0223-5

Please submit comments or report errors to www.sparknotes.com/errors.

Printed and bound in Canada.

Written by Nathan Barber.

SAT is a registered trademark of the College Entrance Examination Board, which was not involved in
the production of and does not endorse this product.

Contents

Contents *DAILY SPARK* *ENGLISH TEST PREP*

Introduction

The *Daily Spark* series gives teachers an easy way to transform downtime into productive time. The 180 exercises—one for each day of the school year—will take students five to ten minutes to complete and can be used at the beginning of class, in the few moments before turning to a new subject, or at the end of class. A full answer key in the back of the book provides detailed explanations of each problem.

The exercises in this book may be photocopied and handed out to the class, projected as a transparency, or even read aloud. In addition to class time use, they can be assigned as homework exercises or extra credit problems.

The SAT is changing, and the *Daily Spark* is a great way to get your students ready for the new multiple-choice questions and Critical Reading section. The *SAT: English Test Prep Daily Spark* gives students lots of practice with all kinds of question types, including Identifying Sentence Errors, Sentence Completions, Reading Comprehension, and Improving Paragraphs.

Spark your students' interest with the *SAT: English Test Prep Daily Spark!*

If there is an error, choose the <u>one underlined part</u> that must be changed to make the sentence correct. If there is no error, choose (E).

Despite the home <u>team's</u> best effort, the <u>visitor's</u> <u>played</u> hard and <u>won</u> by forty points.
                 A   B   C   D

<u>No error</u>.
   E

The <u>new carpenters</u> on the TV design show, <u>who are very knowledgeable in their fields,</u>
     A   B

<u>use</u> many different <u>power tools</u>. <u>No error</u>.
 C   D   E

1

Complete the sentences by choosing the best answers.

The singer's _____ lyrics, which prompted much analysis, turned out to be nothing more than randomly assembled phrases from commercials the singer likes.

(A) sinister
(B) reasonable
(C) cryptic
(D) divergent
(E) divulging

The needle of the pressure gauge indicated that an explosion was _____.

(A) formidable
(B) ostensible
(C) imminent
(D) irreconcilable
(E) diametrical

Read the passage and choose the best answers to the questions that follow it.

(1) America is dependent on foreign oil, a fact that dismays many Americans. (2) Hybrid cars, most of which run on gasoline or diesel and electricity, can help America reduce its dependence on foreign oil. (3) They also reduce pollution. (4) Energy sources like electricity and solar power cut down on the harmful emissions that contribute to allergy-aggravating smog. (5) Lobbyists say that eventually hybrid cars will be just as affordable as gasoline-powered and diesel-powered vehicles. (6) However, the auto industry contends that the cost of research and development of hybrids will drive the price of the product higher than consumers will accept.

Which of the following is true about the author of the passage?
(A) The author is probably sympathetic to the auto industry.
(B) The author is probably in favor of the use of hybrids.
(C) The author is probably annoyed by lobbyists.
(D) The author has probably participated in studies on the effectiveness of hybrid cars.
(E) The author probably knows someone who purchased a hybrid.

The passage implies that many Americans
(A) dislike the fact that the U.S. depends on foreign electricity and solar power
(B) dislike the fact that the U.S. is independent of foreign countries
(C) appreciate the fact that lobbyists are working hard to reduce smog nationwide
(D) disapprove of America's reliance on foreign oil
(E) have test-driven hybrids

Complete the sentences by choosing the best answers.

The _____ workers never held a job for more than a few weeks.
(A) inseparable
(B) transcendent
(C) transient
(D) forthcoming
(E) indispensable

The poor cousin tiptoes around the house with a meek, _____ air.
(A) simplistic
(B) superior
(C) subliminal
(D) subservient
(E) subject

Choose the answer that most improves the <u>underlined portion</u> of the original sentence. If the original sentence does not have an error, choose (A).

The herd of zebras <u>move</u> across the plains of the Serengeti with speed and grace.

(A) move
(B) moves
(C) moved
(D) moving
(E) was moving

There once was a Roman <u>emperor, who,</u> did nothing but sit around all day long and feed the pigeons.

(A) emperor, who,
(B) emperor, whom,
(C) emperor, that,
(D) emperor, which,
(E) emperor who

Read the passage and choose the best answers to the questions that follow it.

(1) It seems that every out-of-work celebrity usually ends up hosting a talk show. (2) Unfortunately, talk show careers usually last only a few months. (3) Usually these celebrity talk shows book other underemployed celebrities to come on as guests. (4) Talk shows often amount to nothing more than bad publicity for the hosts. (5) Therefore, as they say in show business, any publicity (even bad publicity) is good publicity.

Which of the following revisions does the paragraph most need?
(A) Add the word "typically" to sentences 4 and 5.
(B) Delete the word "usually" from several sentences.
(C) Place the last sentence of the paragraph at the beginning of the paragraph.
(D) Change the tense of the verbs to past tense.
(E) Change the tense of the verbs to future tense.

In the context of the paragraph, which of the following revisions does sentence 5 most need?
(A) Replace "Therefore" with "Whatever."
(B) Replace "Therefore" with "Still."
(C) Replace "is" with "was."
(D) Add a colon after "business."
(E) Offset "Therefore" with quotation marks.

© 2004 SparkNotes LLC

Complete the sentences by choosing the best answers.

Frank couldn't tell whether the columnist was being _____, or whether she was serious about her unusual opinions.

(A) arcane

(B) defunct

(C) prolific

(D) expository

(E) sarcastic

The company brought together its best engineers to _____ on a plan that would _____ the performance of many of its products.

(A) collaborate . . . enhance

(B) perforate . . . improve

(C) exasperate . . . deviate

(D) exacerbate . . . confound

(E) enervate . . . advance

7

Read the passage and choose the best answer to the question that follows it.

(1) Nearly all scientists agree that global warming is melting the world's largest glacial structures and causing water levels to rise. (2) Researchers estimate that the earth's water levels, particularly in seas and oceans, rise a fraction of an inch each year. (3) If the ice caps continue to melt, the gulf stream could be affected.

The term "glacial structures" most likely refers to which of the following?
(A) frozen tundra
(B) polar ice caps
(C) mountain ice and snow
(D) intercontinental glaciers
(E) frozen lakes

Improving Sentences

Choose the answer that most improves the <u>underlined portion</u> of the original sentence. If the original sentence does not have an error, choose (A).

Once the expiration date on the milk has passed, it <u>would be prudent to dispose</u> of the old milk.
(A) would be prudent to dispose
(B) would have been prudent to have disposed
(C) would be, prudent to dispose,
(D) was prudent to dispose
(E) might would be prudent to dispose

Jenny's piggy <u>bank, fell</u> from the shelf and shattered into a thousand tiny pieces.
(A) bank, fell
(B) bank, falls
(C) bank falls
(D) bank that fell
(E) bank fell

If there is an error, choose the <u>one underlined part</u> that must be changed to make the sentence correct. If there is no error, choose (E).

The local veterinarian said he <u>won't never</u> do any medical work on an animal <u>larger than</u> a small
                            A   B

horse or small cow <u>because he didn't</u> specialize <u>in that type</u> of medicine in college. <u>No error</u>.
                       C   D   E

Carol <u>bought</u> a <u>brand new</u> blanket <u>for the</u> baby<u>, which was</u> blue.
      A   B   C   D

<u>No error</u>.
  E

Read the passage and choose the best answers to the questions that follow it.

(1) There are many ways to figure out whether you will be successful at a particular endeavor. (2) One way to research the outcomes of other similar endeavors. (3) This could help you determine your odds of success. (4) Therefore, statistics are of only marginal assistance without smart analysis.

In the context of the paragraph, which of the following is the best revision of sentence 2?
(A) One way to research the outcomes of other similar endeavors is:
(B) One way, is to research the outcomes, of other similar endeavors.
(C) One way is to research the outcomes of other similar endeavors.
(D) Some ways are to research the outcomes of other similar endeavors.
(E) One way perhaps to research the outcomes of other similar endeavors.

Which of the following revisions does sentence 4 most need?
(A) Replace "Therefore" with "Perhaps."
(B) Replace "Therefore" with "However."
(C) Offset "without smart analysis" with commas.
(D) Replace "are" with "were."
(E) Remove the comma after "Therefore."

Read the passage and choose the best answer to the question that follows it.

(1) If I could travel back in time and found any company or industry, I would choose the bottled water industry. (2) This industry has a brilliant strategy: take water that costs a few pennies, bottle it in plastic containers that cost a few pennies, and then sell it for about a dollar a bottle. (3) That is pure genius. (4) The best part is that many bottled waters are actually *dirtier* than tap water. (5) But because of clever marketing campaigns, most people think all bottled water comes from the purest mountain streams.

Which of the following is the main idea of the paragraph?
(A) Consumers are so naive that industries often take advantage of them.
(B) The bottled water industry has a brilliant business plan.
(C) The author would like to buy stock in bottled water companies.
(D) The bottled water industry should be prosecuted.
(E) The bottled water that most people enjoy is exactly the same as tap water in both taste and content.

Complete the sentences by choosing the best answers.

The witness's statement originally seemed devastating for the defense, but things looked up when she _____ on Thursday.

(A) recanted
(B) recounted
(C) reminisced
(D) reminded
(E) revisited

Despite the many _____ that greet each new novel he publishes, Mr. King remains remarkably _____.

(A) awards . . . pompous
(B) accolades . . . humble
(C) admonitions . . . pessimistic
(D) honors . . . haughty
(E) criticisms . . . defeated

13

If there is an error, choose the <u>one underlined part</u> that must be changed to make the sentence correct. If there is no error, choose (E).

Bess <u>will mail</u> the package to her cousin <u>in Atlanta</u> fourteen long <u>days before</u> the fragile
     A   B   C

package <u>arrived</u>. <u>No error</u>.
        D   E

Video games <u>have gotten</u> more and more realistic <u>every year</u>; when I <u>was</u> a kid, for
        A   B   C

example, the most high-tech game <u>is</u> Pac-Man. <u>No error</u>.
                            D   E

Read the passage and choose the best answer to the question that follows it.

(1) The local library has requested a fifteen percent increase in its budget for next year. (2) Without the additional funds, according to a library spokesperson, the library will not be able to expand its collection of literature. (3) Many people say that before the budget is approved, the community should be allowed to vote on the use of the funds. (4) Others oppose the increase because they argue that the growth of the local library will affect local merchants who sell books. (5) If local merchants lose sales, they say, the town will lose tax revenues, and everyone will suffer.

Based on the information in the passage, which of the following conclusions can be drawn?
(A) Local business owners do not support the library
(B) The library wants to buy more books.
(C) The fifteen percent budgetary increase is relatively small.
(D) The fifteen percent budgetary increase is relatively high.
(E) The city's budget could be devastated because of a loss of revenue from local bookstores.

Complete the sentences by choosing the best answers.

After listening to the prisoner's passionate pleas, Judge Jim decided to grant the man _____.
(A) platitude
(B) vengeance
(C) vulnerability
(D) viscosity
(E) clemency

The _____ clues were discovered when the famous detective conducted a _____ investigation.
(A) unmistakable . . . enthusiastic
(B) mysterious . . . meticulous
(C) shrouded . . . thorough
(D) hidden . . . thorough
(E) faint . . . painstaking

Choose the answer that most improves the <u>underlined portion</u> of the original sentence. If the original sentence does not have an error, choose (A).

She thought she had bought temporary dye<u>; therefore, her hair</u> was bright orange for three months, so it seemed she'd made a mistake.
(A) ; therefore, her hair
(B) ; and, her hair
(C) , and, her hair
(D) ; thus, her hair
(E) , but her hair

<u>Dogs are man's best friend</u>, except when the dog scratches the sofa or soils the carpet.
(A) Dogs are man's best friend
(B) Dogs are men's best friend
(C) Dogs are man's best friends
(D) Dogs were man's best friend
(E) A dog is man's best friend

Read the passage and choose the best answer to the question that follows it.

(1) Meteorological technology has progressed in leaps and bounds in the last half-century. (2) Meteorologists today have access to instruments that scientists of days past could only dream of. (3) They use information gathered by satellites, airplanes, and high-tech gadgets and gizmos placed around the world. (4) In recent years, the technology of meteorology has improved, the science of meteorology has evolved, but one thing remains the same.

Based on the rest of the paragraph, which of the following is the best choice for the final sentence of the paragraph?
(A) Therefore, meteorology must be the most precise science of the last half-century.
(B) The ability to predict the weather must also be improving.
(C) The weather is still unpredictable.
(D) The weather has changed over the last half-century, too, so the science of meteorology must continue to change.
(E) Weather forecasters should return to school to earn their degrees in meteorology.

Sentence Completions

Complete the sentences by choosing the best answers.

The keynote speaker began his address with a humorous _____ that was _____ to his presentation.

(A) anachronism . . . fortuitous
(B) abbreviation . . . conditional
(C) aberration . . . instructional
(D) anomaly . . . enigmatic
(E) anecdote . . . relevant

The computer and software _____ donated more than a million dollars to the ASPCA.

(A) peon
(B) panhandler
(C) pauper
(D) typhoon
(E) magnate

Improving Paragraphs

Read the passage and choose the best answer to the question that follows it.

(1) Sunnydale High was very proud of its standardized test scores, which have risen steadily over the last ten years. (2) In contrast, test scores have actually declined in some school districts in the area. (3) Sunnydale's rising scores are evidence that Sunnydale High is doing a better job of educating students than other schools in the area. (4) The test scores also reflect well on the teachers.

Which revision does sentence 1 most need?
(A) Replace "was" with "had been."
(B) Replace "was" with "is."
(C) Add "which" after "Sunnydale High."
(D) Add "that" after Sunnydale High.
(E) Replace "its" with "their."

Identifying Sentence Errors

If there is an error, select the <u>one underlined part</u> that must be changed to make the sentence correct. If there is no error, choose (E).

The <u>Joneses'</u> schnauzer barked <u>wildly</u> <u>inside</u> <u>her</u> doghouse. <u>No error.</u>
     A   B   C   D   E

The amateur hockey players <u>who are going</u> to <u>try out for</u> the Olympics in a few
                            A   B

weeks <u>includes</u> <u>several local superstars</u>. <u>No error.</u>
      C   D   E

Read the passage and choose the best answers to the questions that follow it.

(1) Computer technology is advancing so quickly that computer users can hardly keep up without spending lots of money. (2) When someone purchases a top-of-the-line computer, he can be sure that after only a few weeks, his new computer will no longer be cutting-edge. (3) A computer that cost over a thousand dollars ten years ago would probably fetch only a few dollars at a garage sale today. (4) Companies often stop providing tech support for programs that are only a few years old, making them even more impractical.

Which of the following is the main idea of the passage?
(A) There is no point in buying a computer.
(B) Computers are smart investments for people hoping to resell them at a profit.
(C) Rapid advances in computer technology make it hard to stay up-to-date.
(D) The cost of computers does not equal the power of computers.
(E) It's best to shop for computers at garage sales.

Which of the following would be the best conclusion for the passage?
(A) People determined to stay up-to-date should be ready to spend quite a bit of money.
(B) Buying computers is largely impractical.
(C) People should purchase top-of-the-line computers if they can.
(D) Someone who wanted to open a computer store would make millions if she sold new technology at low prices.
(E) Someone insistent on buying a computer should expect to either spend a fortune or be stuck with inferior technology.

If there is an error, choose the <u>one underlined part</u> that must be changed to make the sentence correct. If there is no error, choose (E).

The morning exercise class and <u>the afternoon yoga class</u> <u>attracted</u> so many

                                             A   B

<u>participants</u> that the manager of the health club <u>was forced</u> to hire another exercise

     C   D

instructor and another yoga instructor. <u>No error</u>.

                                              E

<u>One</u> of the main reasons cities <u>have begun enforcing</u> bans on smoking <u>are</u> to protect

 A   B   C

the health of those who do not smoke <u>and to reduce</u> air pollution. <u>No error</u>.

                                                D   E

Read the passage and choose the best answers to the questions that follow it.

(1) The spirit of competition is often the ostensible reason that high schools offer competitive extracurricular activities. (2) However, one might argue that competitive activities really exist to generate revenue for the school and promote its name. (3) Sports like football and basketball draw thousands of people to the stands each year, generating profits for the school. (4) Other competitive activities, such as debate, showcase students for colleges and universities. (5) Such competitions are nothing more than free advertisement and shameless self-promotion for schools.

The author of the paragraph above can best be described as which of the following?
(A) supportive of competitive extracurricular activities
(B) cynical about the legitimacy of the results of competitions
(C) supportive of schools' motivations for sponsoring competitive extracurricular activities
(D) cynical about schools' motivations for sponsoring competitive extracurricular activities
(E) ambivalent about the role of competitive extracurricular activities

In sentence 1, "ostensible" means
(A) subversive
(B) submersed
(C) apparent
(D) contradictory
(E) without reservation

Identifying Sentence Errors

If there is an error, choose the <u>one underlined part</u> that must be changed to make the sentence correct. If there is no error, choose (E).

The new deli<u>, on the corner with the great pastrami sandwiches,</u> <u>gets</u> many of <u>its</u>
                           A   B   C

customers from the office building <u>across the street</u>. <u>No error</u>.
                                        D   E

Maggie <u>ran</u> down the stairs, <u>darted</u> out the door, tripped <u>over the skateboard,</u> and <u>scrapes</u>
     A   B   C   D

her knee on the hard concrete. <u>No error</u>.
                                  E

Choose the answer that most improves the <u>underlined portion</u> of the original sentence. If the original sentence does not have an error, choose (A).

<u>Sometimes the house gets so disorganized and messy; we</u> need a professional cleaning crew.
(A) Sometimes the house gets so disorganized and messy; we
(B) Sometimes the house gets so disorganized and messy: we
(C) Sometimes the house gets so disorganized and messy. We
(D) Sometimes the house gets so disorganized and messy because we
(E) Sometimes the house gets so disorganized and messy that we

My uncle played baseball in the minor leagues <u>not only in the United States and in Japan</u>.
(A) not only in the United States and in Japan
(B) not only in the United States after in Japan
(C) not only in the United States and in Japan in addition
(D) not only in the United States but also in Japan
(E) not only just in the United States but also in Japan, too

DAILY SPARK ENGLISH TEST PREP

Improving Paragraphs

Read the passage and choose the best answers to the questions that follow it.

(1) Before steam engines were used in the construction of railroads, railroad workers put down track by hand and then hammered the spikes. (2) According to legend, a man named John Henry could drive spikes faster than any other worker. (3) Eventually technology improved. (4) Steam power was applied to a device that drove spikes. (5) Promoters arranged for John Henry to compete in a railroad-spike-driving contest against the steam-powered device. (6) Ultimately, John Henry wins the competition.

Which of the following sentences is the best combination of sentence 3 and sentence 4?
(A) Eventually the technology was applied to the device that improved spike driving.
(B) The spike-driving device eventually improved as the technology improved and steam power was applied.
(C) Technology improved, and a steam-powered device to drive spikes was invented.
(D) As the spike-driving device became steam-powered, technology eventually evolved.
(E) As steam technology eventually improved, spike-driving technology was applied.

Which of the following revisions does sentence 6 most need?
(A) Replace "wins" with "won."
(B) Replace "wins" with "will win."
(C) Remove the comma after "Ultimately."
(D) Replace "Ultimately" with "Therefore."
(E) Replace "Ultimately" with "Additionally."

Complete the sentences by choosing the best answers.

The scholar believed it was his duty to _____ the masses by telling them about his revolutionary _____.
(A) deprecate . . . enigma
(B) incarcerate . . . policy
(C) subjugate . . . jargon
(D) enlighten . . . doctrine
(E) dominate . . . proselytized

The career counselor says that in the current economy, it is _____ to apply for several jobs instead of holding out for the ideal job.
(A) reprehensible
(B) gratifying
(C) prudent
(D) indispensable
(E) audacious

Reading Comprehension

Read the passage and choose the best answers to the questions that follow it.

(1) Some people complain that film actors make too much money. (2) What these people don't understand is that most actors are worth their exorbitant salaries. (3) Even terrible movies can be salvaged by a great actor in a lead or supporting role, so it's no wonder that top actors command millions of dollars per movie. (4) If a movie that costs $150 million to make grosses $225 million because Hollywood's hottest leading man starred in it, that leading man's $5 million salary was a great investment. (5) People who complain about highly paid professionals like actors and actresses simply haven't thought about the economics of making a hit film.

One can infer from the passage that great actors
(A) have a fair market value of $5 million
(B) can overcome flawed scripts
(C) pale in comparison to state-of-the-art special effects
(D) have no effect on average-income consumers
(E) drive hard-working people away from theaters

The author of the passage implies that those people who object to actors' high salaries
(A) rarely go to the movies
(B) are jealous of the actors' wealth
(C) misunderstand the lifestyles actors must lead
(D) lack the business sense to comprehend the actors' true value
(E) have no way of comprehending what $5 million can buy

If there is an error, choose the <u>one underlined part</u> that must be changed to make the sentence correct. If there is no error, choose (E).

<u>Me and her</u> <u>went</u> to dinner, to the movies, to the coffee shop, <u>and then to the lake</u> <u>to watch</u>
  A   B   C   D

the sunrise. <u>No error</u>.
                 E

The scientist <u>was flabbergasted</u> when he <u>read</u> the final report, which <u>verified that</u> the
                        A   B   C

element was made of <u>string cheese</u>. <u>No error</u>.
                            D   E

Complete the sentences by choosing the best answers.

The residents of the _____ region performed a rain dance and were rewarded with a _____.

(A) parched . . . heat
(B) scorched . . . validation
(C) saturated . . . monsoon
(D) arid . . . deluge
(E) barren . . . consecration

The waitstaff always fights to serve Ms. Pratt, an extravagant tipper who is famous for her _____.

(A) miserliness
(B) efficiency
(C) deliberation
(D) largess
(E) consternation

Choose the answer that most improves the <u>underlined portion</u> of the original sentence. If the original sentence does not have an error, choose (A).

<u>Determine</u> to make his mark in the business world, Larry went to grad school to get his M.B.A.
(A) Determine
(B) Determination
(C) By determining
(D) Because of determining
(E) Determined

Remember that movie stars, however snotty and bratty they are now, <u>was once a regular person</u> just like everyone else.
(A) was once a regular person
(B) were once a regular person
(C) was once regular people
(D) once, as a regular person,
(E) were once regular people

DAILY SPARK ENGLISH TEST PREP

Read the passage and choose the best answers to the questions that follow it.

(1) Despite the relative reluctance of Americans to adopt it, soccer is the most popular sport in the world and has been for several decades. (2) Soccer, which is called "football" in most places, has few rules compared with such sports as baseball. (3) Also, in contrast to baseball and American football, soccer games have few pauses in the action. (4) Soccer scores aren't as high as scores are in American sports, but many people consider that an exciting feature of the game, because the occasional goals are that much more thrilling.

Which of the following is true of the paragraph?
(A) The author likes soccer.
(B) The author is not an American.
(C) The author presents the information in an objective manner.
(D) The author is biased against American sports.
(E) The author is biased against soccer.

Which of the following is the main idea of the passage?
(A) Soccer is more popular in Europe than American football is.
(B) Soccer is a great sport, despite its unpopularity in America.
(C) Baseball and basketball will need overhauls if they are to compete on the world stage with soccer.
(D) Soccer is an all-around better sport than any other in the world.
(E) Soccer is the simplest sport in the world.

If there is an error, choose the <u>one underlined part</u> that must be changed to make the sentence correct. If there is no error, choose (E).

People <u>shouldn't never</u> pump gas while a <u>car's</u> engine <u>is running,</u> because of the possibility
       A   B   C

<u>of a spark</u> causing a fire. <u>No error</u>.
  D   E

When Alicia <u>arrived</u> home, she found that the dogs <u>had got</u> <u>into</u> the trash and <u>spilled it</u>
         A   B C   D

everywhere. <u>No error</u>.
        E

Choose the answer that most improves the <u>underlined portion</u> of the original sentence. If the original sentence does not have an error, choose (A).

I had a dream that I turned into a cartoon character and a guy with an eraser <u>had chased</u> me for hours.

(A) had chased
(B) have chased
(C) did chase
(D) chased
(E) has chased

Silent movies use <u>music, actors'</u> expressions to convey emotions.

(A) music, actors'
(B) music, along with actors'
(C) music, together with actors'
(D) music but actors'
(E) music and actors'

Read the passage and choose the best answers to the questions that follow it.

(1) College tuitions are soaring, leaving many parents wondering if they will be able to afford higher education for their children. (2) Cutbacks in government aid combined with skyrocketing tuition are making it unfeasible even for families of moderate wealth to fully fund their children's educations. (3) In America, people say that you can be anything you want to be. (4) But getting an education is crucial if you hope to achieve the American dream.

With which of the following statements would the author of this passage most likely agree?
(A) The government should help students pay for college.
(B) The cost of a college education is unreasonable.
(C) Borrowing money for college may be the answer to rising education costs.
(D) An education is not necessary to succeed in America.
(E) High school students should think twice about going to college.

In sentence 2, the word "unfeasible" means
(A) possible
(B) unworkable
(C) indescribable
(D) indiscernible
(E) irreconcilable

DAILY SPARK ENGLISH TEST PREP

Improving Sentences

Choose the answer that most improves the <u>underlined portion</u> of the original sentence. If the original sentence does not have an error, choose (A).

Some of the most beautiful fish in the world are found <u>not in neither the Caribbean or the Mediterranean</u> but rather in my aquarium.

(A) not in neither the Caribbean or the Mediterranean
(B) not in either the Caribbean nor the Mediterranean
(C) not in neither the Caribbean nor the Mediterranean
(D) in neither the Caribbean or the Mediterranean
(E) neither in the Caribbean nor in the Mediterranean

The teacher always <u>told the class that their's no such thing</u> as a stupid question.

(A) told the class that their's no such thing
(B) told the class that their wasn't no such thing
(C) told the class that theirs no such thing
(D) told the class that there is no such thing
(E) told the class that there were no such things

Complete the sentences by choosing the best answers.

The priest's _____ approach to the dilemma made sense even to the most confirmed _____.

(A) enigmatic . . . optimist
(B) reluctant . . . participant
(C) influential . . . observer
(D) sporadic . . . cynic
(E) pragmatic . . . skeptic

The _____ violinist has been amazing audiences since she was thirteen years old.
(A) financier
(B) tycoon
(C) philanthropist
(D) recluse
(E) virtuoso

Read the passage and choose the best answers to the questions that follow it.

(1) When television writers get stuck for ideas, they always seem to turn to the same old gimmicks. (2) One such gimmick is to get the main characters stuck somewhere, perhaps in an elevator, on an island, or on a plane that is going down. (3) The plot always unfolds in the same way: the characters reveal all sorts of intimate information, only to be rescued before the show ends. (4) Perhaps the most overused gimmick is the introduction of a celebrity into the cast of characters as someone's relative or love interest. (5) This move is a sure sign that the writers and producers have run out of fresh material.

Which of the following conclusions can be made based on the passage?
(A) TV writers and producers enjoy using gimmicks.
(B) TV writers and producers all suffer from writer's block.
(C) TV writers and producers sometimes succeed in persuading celebrities to appear on shows.
(D) TV audiences cannot recognize a plot that is used in a multitude of settings and genres.
(E) TV writers and producers are not nearly as creative as they often appear to be.

Which of the following inferences can be made based on the passage?
(A) A small group of writers and producers write the material for most TV shows.
(B) Using formulas is not the way to create successful TV shows.
(C) There are only three main scenarios that writers use to invigorate shows.
(D) Storylines must always feature original, never-before-seen content if a show is to be successful.
(E) Certain scenarios and storylines are used in many kinds of shows.

If there is an error, choose the <u>one underlined part</u> that must be changed to make the sentence correct. If there is no error, choose (E).

His claim to fame is <u>because</u> he <u>was</u> once on a reality TV <u>show; however,</u> he got kicked off
             A   B   C   D

the show after the first episode. <u>No error</u>.
                           E

<u>Its</u> amazing how moviegoers <u>willingly</u> pay the exorbitant prices for popcorn, candy,
A   B

<u>soda, and nachos</u> <u>at the theater</u>. <u>No error</u>.
     C   D   E

Choose the answer that most improves the <u>underlined portion</u> of the original sentence. If the original sentence does not have an error, choose (A).

Extra security <u>was hired</u> by the colleges for the football game.

(A) Extra security was hired by the colleges for the football game.
(B) Extra security were hired by the colleges for the football game.
(C) Extra security was hired for the football game by the colleges.
(D) The colleges hired extra security for the football game.
(E) The colleges were hired by extra security for the football game.

She broke her <u>nails trying to open the can of soda which had just been painted a beautiful shade of cherry red</u>.

(A) nails trying to open the can of soda which had just been painted a beautiful shade of cherry red
(B) nails, which had just been painted a beautiful shade of cherry red, trying to open the can of soda
(C) nails which had just been painted, trying to open the can of soda, a beautiful shade of cherry red
(D) nails while trying to open the can of soda which had just been painted a beautiful shade of cherry red
(E) nails trying to open the can of soda, which had just been painted a beautiful shade of cherry red

Read the passage and choose the best answers to the questions that follow it.

(1) Customers can accumulate points for using the ChargeMe credit card and then use those points to purchase great merchandise. (2) Points can even be used to go on a vacation to the Bahamas the Caribbean or Florida. (3) The marketing division of ChargeMe hopes that this points program will not only encourage existing customers to use their cards more; but will also actually encourage others to apply for a ChargeMe credit card.

Which of the following is the best revision of sentence 2?

(A) Points can even be used to go on a vacation to: the Bahamas the Caribbean or Florida

(B) Points can even be used to go on a vacation to; the Bahamas the Caribbean the Virgin Islands or the British Isles

(C) Points perhaps can possibly even be used to go on a vacation

(D) Points can even be used to go on a vacation to the Bahamas, the Caribbean, or Florida

(E) Points can even be used to go on a vacation to the Bahamas; the Caribbean; or Florida

Which revision does sentence 3 most need?

(A) Replace "but will actually" with "but may actually."

(B) Remove the semicolon between "more" and "but."

(C) Replace "encourage" with "encourages."

(D) Remove "also."

(E) Add a comma after "points program."

Read the passage and choose the best answers to the questions that follow it.

(1) The Barton County School District plans to launch a new program for evaluating its teachers. (2) BCSD is hoping that its pilot program can serve as a prototype for other districts across the state and even across the country. (3) The committee wants its evaluation program to measure a teacher's knowledge of his or her subject matter, effectiveness in the classroom, and demeanor in and out of the classroom.

Besides evaluating each teacher in the district, BCSD also hopes to do which of the following with its teacher evaluation program?
(A) offer the program as a model for other interested administrators
(B) determine teacher merit pay
(C) determine student placement based on teacher competency
(D) place teachers in suitable schools
(E) measure the relative intelligence of the district teachers

Which of the following will not be measured by the BCSD teacher evaluation program?
(A) a teacher's manner in a classroom setting
(B) a teacher's efficacy with students in a learning environment
(C) a teacher's behavior and conduct outside the classroom
(D) a teacher's comprehension of his or her main subject
(E) a teacher's expertise in cross-curricular subjects

Complete the sentences by choosing the best answers.

The teacher's scribbled _____ not only excited Sida, they _____ her to keep up her hard work.

(A) complements . . . motivated
(B) compliments . . . motivated
(C) exhortations . . . exhilarated
(D) conflagrations . . . enervated
(E) dissertations . . . ameliorated

Much to the dismay of the scientific community, the _____ supported a theory that completely _____ fifty years of accepted science.

(A) orator . . . collaborated
(B) recluse . . . embroiled
(C) prophet . . . disoriented
(D) novice . . . discredited
(E) evangelist . . . disregarded

DAILY SPARK ENGLISH TEST PREP

© 2004 SparkNotes LLC

Identifying Sentence Errors

If there is an error, choose the <u>one underlined part</u> that must be changed to make the sentence correct. If there is no error, choose (E).

All the <u>people in the office</u> overlooking the lake <u>needs</u> to be sure that their
　　　　　　A　　　　　　　　　　　　　　　　　　　B

<u>computers are</u> turned off <u>before they leave</u> work on Friday. <u>No error</u>.
　　C　　　　　　　　　　　D　　　　　　　　　　　　　E

Louis <u>couldn't overcome</u> the embarrassment <u>of spilling</u> grape soda on <u>they're</u> carpet,
　　　　A　　　　　　　　　　　　　　　B　　　　　　　　　　C

<u>so he left</u> immediately. <u>No error</u>.
　D　　　　　　　　　　E

Read the passage and choose the best answers to the questions that follow it.

(1) Less than one percent of the money in the criminal justice system budget is spent on vocational training for inmates in state prisons. (2) Critics argue that if more money was spent on training, fewer prisoners would return to a life of crime. (3) If more money was spent on helping prisoners learn work skills, less money would have to be spent on processing and incarcerating convicts. (4) This is assuming, of course, that inmates want vocational training.

Which of the following inferences can be made based on the argument in the passage above?
(A) Inmates who receive vocational training will probably wind up back in prison.
(B) Inmates who receive vocational training are just as likely to commit crimes as those who do not receive vocational training.
(C) Inmates who receive vocational training are less likely to commit crimes upon their release.
(D) Tax money should not be spent on vocational training for inmates.
(E) The criminal justice system should reevaluate its priorities.

In sentence 3, the term "incarcerating" means
(A) setting free
(B) educating
(C) prosecuting
(D) imprisoning
(E) releasing

Read the passage and choose the best answer to the question that follows it.

(1) Frank decided to open his own construction company. (2) His first move was to hire a crew. (3) He hired a carpenter. (4) He hired a plumber. (5) He hired an electrician and a concrete expert. (6) Frank wanted to advertise, so he put an ad in the newspaper and he ran the ad for three months. (7) Within a matter of just a few weeks, Frank had signed twelve contracts for new housing construction in three different subdivisions in of the city. (8) Frank was well on his way to success.

Which of the following is the best combination of sentences 2, 3, 4, and 5?

(A) Frank's first move was to: hire a crew, hire a carpenter, hire an electrician, and hire a concrete expert.

(B) Frank, as his first move, was to hire a crew that consisted of everything from a carpenter to a concrete expert.

(C) Frank's first move was to hire a crew consisting of a carpenter, a plumber, an electrician, and a concrete expert.

(D) A carpenter, a plumber, an electrician, and a concrete expert made up Frank's crew; he hired them.

(E) Frank first hired a carpenter, a plumber, an electrician, and then a concrete expert as his first move for a crew.

DAILYSPARK ENGLISH TEST PREP

Choose the answer that most improves the <u>underlined portion</u> of the original sentence. If the original sentence does not have an error, choose (A).

Bull riders <u>must surely have to really be</u> strong and brave.
(A) must surely have to really be
(B) surely must really have to be
(C) really must surely be
(D) have to surely be
(E) have to be

Doctors and <u>nurses, that work in emergency rooms,</u> often suffer from work-related stress.
(A) nurses, that work in emergency rooms,
(B) nurses who work in emergency rooms
(C) nurses which, work in emergency rooms,
(D) nurses, who work, in emergency rooms
(E) nurses, whom work in emergency rooms,

DAILY SPARK ENGLISH TEST PREP

Read the passage and choose the best answers to the questions that follow it.

(1) All humans need sleep in order to function on a day-to-day basis. (2) Some people need eight to ten hours of sleep each night, while other people need only four to six hours of sleep. (3) Some people like to stay up very late; others prefer to go to bed early so they can wake up early. (4) While many people like to sleep on firm mattresses, others enjoy soft mattresses. (5) Clearly, there are as many variations of "a good night's sleep" as there are people who sleep.

In the context of the paragraph, which of the following revisions does sentence 1 most need?
(A) Add "However" to the beginning of the sentence.
(B) Replace "day-to-day" with "daily."
(C) Replace "All humans need" with "Every human needs."
(D) Offset the phrase "in order to function" with commas.
(E) Replace "basis" with "basic."

In which of the following places in the paragraph should the following sentence be added?
However, not all humans have the same sleep habits, preferences, and needs.
(A) Add to the beginning of the paragraph
(B) Add between sentence 1 and sentence 2
(C) Add between sentence 3 and sentence 4
(D) Add to the end of the paragraph
(E) Combine with sentence 5

Complete the sentences by choosing the best answers.

The new governor never _____ any of his campaign promises, and as a result his supporters felt totally _____.
(A) made . . . convinced
(B) encouraged . . . secure
(C) authored . . . bamboozled
(D) fulfilled . . . betrayed
(E) authenticated . . . disassociated

Sam idolized his brother and tried to _____ him in every respect.
(A) vindicate
(B) emulate
(C) propagate
(D) formulate
(E) integrate

Read the passage and choose the best answers to the questions that follow it.

(1) Some people enjoy old black-and-white movies, some enjoy science fiction shows, and others are addicted to reality TV. (2) I love infomercials. (3) I plan to build a website devoted solely to the infomercial. (4) My dream is to one day open an Infomercial Museum and Hall of Fame. (5) Despite what people say, I have not developed an unhealthy obsession with the products advertised in infomercials. (6) I'm fully aware that most of the products showcased on infomercials are junk. (7) I am interested primarily in infomercial marketing techniques, the salesmanship of the D-list celebrities who endorse the products, and the crazy gimmicks that manufacturers use to try to sell their goods. (8) Sales execs and ad agencies could learn a lot from the geniuses behind infomercials.

Which of the following is implied in the passage?
(A) The author has collected an impressive collection of vintage infomercial products.
(B) The author has accumulated a sizable debt because of an addiction to infomercial products.
(C) People have made fun of the author for his interest in infomercials.
(D) The author never watches infomercials; he just records them.
(E) The author must be very wealthy, if he intends to open an infomercial museum.

Which of the following words best describes the author's account of his interest in infomercials?
(A) contentious
(B) contemporary
(C) convoluted
(D) candid
(E) condescending

Read the passage and choose the best answers to the questions that follow it.

(1) After World War II, several nations joined forces and creating the United Nations. (2) The U.N. created an eleven-member security council charged with handling threats to world peace. (3) The idea that the maintenance of world peace would rest with all the major powers certainly was a lofty goal. (4) Probably, the goal has never come to fruition. (5) As a result, many critics argue that the U.N. is really just a passive organization that does little to bring about world peace.

Which of the following is the best revision of sentence 1?
(A) After World War II, several nations joining forces and creating the United Nations.
(B) After World War II, several nations joined forces and created the United Nations.
(C) After World War II, several nations were joining forces and had created the United Nations.
(D) After World War II, several nations had joined forces and were creating the United Nations.
(E) After World War II, several nations joined and created forces and the United Nations.

In the context of the paragraph, which revision does sentence 4 most need?
(A) Replace "has" with "may never have."
(B) Replace "Probably" with "Unfortunately."
(C) Remove the comma after "Probably."
(D) Make "goal" plural.
(E) Add "to" after "has."

Identifying Sentence Errors

If there is an error, choose the <u>one underlined part</u> that must be changed to make the sentence correct. If there is no error, choose (E).

With the expanded use of email, <u>it is</u> very possible that <u>in the future</u> the world <u>had lost</u>
                              A   B   C

the will and desire <u>to write letters</u> the old-fashioned way. <u>No error</u>.
                   D   E

When I look <u>in the mirror</u> I <u>saw</u> a person <u>who has goals</u> and who plans on reaching those
           A   B   C

goals <u>through hard work, determination,</u> and desire. <u>No error</u>.
          D   E

Choose the answer that most improves the <u>underlined portion</u> of the original sentence. If the original sentence does not have an error, choose (A).

The professor stood in front of the class of college freshmen <u>and lectures them</u> on punctuality, discipline, and responsibility.
(A) and lectures them
(B) and, lectures them
(C) and, lectured them
(D) and lectured them
(E) and lectured their

Manny and Miguel spent all <u>night; playing</u> their guitars, talking, and writing new music.
(A) night; playing
(B) night playing
(C) night: playing
(D) night and were playing
(E) nights playing

Reading Comprehension

Read the passage and choose the best answers to the questions that follow it.

(1) Insurance companies fleece millions and millions of customers each year. (2) They charge people thousands of dollars annually. (3) If a customer has an accident, the company pays for only a portion of the expenses. (4) Furthermore, the insurance company raises the cost of the customer's insurance policy every time he or she makes a claim. (5) There must be something unethical about this practice.

Which of the following is the main idea of the passage?
(A) People don't really need insurance.
(B) The government should intervene to help insurance customers.
(C) Insurance companies owe it to their customers to process their claims in an efficient manner.
(D) Insurance companies operate illegally.
(E) Insurance companies' business practices are unscrupulous.

Based on the context of the passage, the word "fleece" in sentence 1 means
(A) swindle
(B) cover
(C) aid
(D) develop
(E) insure

Read the passage and choose the best answers to the questions that follow it.

(1) People often assume that the eagle was the natural and obvious choice to be the national bird of the United States. (2) However, Ben Franklin, one of the nation's founding fathers, had another bird in mind: the turkey. (3) Franklin believed the turkey is a powerful bird that represents America well. (4) The turkey didn't catch on as the national bird, despite his best efforts. (5) If Franklin's bid had been successful, Thanksgiving would be celebrated differently than it is today.

Which of the following is the best revision of sentence 3?
(A) Franklin believes the turkey is a powerful bird that represents America well.
(B) Franklin believed the turkey was a powerful bird that represents America well.
(C) Franklin believed the turkey was a powerful bird that represented America well.
(D) Franklin believed the turkey is a powerful bird that represented America well.
(E) Franklin believes the turkey is a powerful bird that represented America well.

In the context of the paragraph, which of the following revisions does sentence 4 most need?
(A) Replace "didn't" with "couldn't."
(B) Place the phrase "despite his best efforts" at the beginning of the sentence.
(C) Replace the comma with a semicolon.
(D) Replace "his" with "Franklin's."
(E) Replace "despite" with "in spite of."

DAILY SPARK ENGLISH TEST PREP

© 2004 SparkNotes LLC

Sentence Completions

Complete the sentences by choosing the best answers.

In an attempt to _____ the uprising, the government _____ troops to the frontier.
(A) confess . . . employed
(B) digress . . . convoyed
(C) regress . . . conveyed
(D) suppress . . . deployed
(E) fortress . . . alloyed

The _____ team bounced back from the loss and went on to win the title.
(A) efficient
(B) considerate
(C) resilient
(D) influential
(E) salubrious

Read the passage and choose the best answers to the questions that follow it.

(1) America's Mars exploration cost hundreds of millions of dollars. (2) To date, we have uncovered no firm evidence of life beyond Earth. (3) I think that such an investment is hardly worthwhile, considering the problems we have here on Earth. (4) Shouldn't we spend our tax dollars on education, defense, and the arts instead of worrying about remote reaches of the solar system? (5) I can't understand what proponents of space exploration are thinking.

Which of the following does the author of this passage believe?
(A) Space exploration is too expensive.
(B) Money spent on space exploration is creating a budget deficit.
(C) Money spent on space exploration is driving up the tax rate.
(D) Money spent on space exploration would be better spent on other projects.
(E) Money spent on understanding the universe prevents scientists from understanding the earth.

In sentence 5, the term "proponents" means
(A) advocates
(B) antagonists
(C) scientists
(D) investors
(E) researchers

DAILY SPARK ENGLISH TEST PREP

Sentence Completions

Complete the sentences by choosing the best answers.

Nearly every month, the magazine publishes _____ articles that stir up controversy and enrage half of the magazine's readership.
(A) sensitive
(B) provocative
(C) salutary
(D) prosaic
(E) innocuous

The cheerful letter Angel sent from the front lines of battle did nothing to _____ his mother's fears.
(A) deconstruct
(B) absolve
(C) assuage
(D) defer
(E) incite

Choose the answer that most improves the <u>underlined portion</u> of the original sentence. If the original sentence does not have an error, choose (A).

<u>Soap operas which</u> seem all the same to me, are full of melodrama, secrets, and romance.
(A) Soap operas which
(B) Soap operas: which
(C) Soap operas, which
(D) Soap operas who
(E) Soap operas that

<u>Clothes from the seventies seems</u> to have made a big comeback.
(A) Clothes from the seventies seems
(B) Clothes from the seventies seem
(C) Clothes from the seventies had seemed
(D) Clothes, from the seventies, seems
(E) Clothes from the seventies seemingly

Read the passage and choose the best answers to the questions that follow it.

(1) In the past few decades, scientists have made remarkable headway in such endeavors as cancer research, epidemiology, and genetics. (2) Animal rights activists often protest the use of animals in scientific research. (3) However, to protest experimentation on lab animals is to protest progress itself. (4) If not for the animals used for decades in labs around the world, cures would go undiscovered and diseases would go untreated. (5) Scientists and researchers would never be able to conduct potentially dangerous experiments on humans.

Based on the passage, one can infer that
(A) animals have no rights
(B) animals are not protected under the laws of any countries
(C) scientists do nothing to harm the animals in labs
(D) the author believes strongly in the necessity of research on lab animals
(E) the author is making an ironic argument in support of animal activists

According to the author, which of the following might be a possible consequence of the discontinuation of research on laboratory animals?
(A) the inhibition of progress
(B) the use of plants and fish in lieu of lab animals
(C) the loss of many research jobs around the world
(D) a resurgence of protests from anti-animal rights activists
(E) the unlawful harming of many humans in underdeveloped nations

Read the passage and choose the best answers to the questions that follow it.

(1) My grandfather frequently rode trains from place to place when he was a young boy. (2) Occasionally he paid for his passage, but more often than not, he hopped inside an empty boxcar and hitched a ride from town to town. (3) He has worked on his train collection for nearly forty years now. (4) He has collected seventy complete train sets, dozens of antique signs, and miscellaneous train and railroad memorabilia. (5) He was even thinking about opening a railroad museum here in town.

Which of the following sentences should be added to the beginning of sentence 3?
(A) His memories of trains are still with him.
(B) Collecting trains can be very expensive.
(C) Collecting trains can be very profitable.
(D) Trains are very collectible.
(E) His memories of riding trains inspired my grandfather to collect trains and train memorabilia.

In the context of the passage, which of the following is the best revision of sentence 5?
(A) He had even thought about opening a railroad museum here in town.
(B) He had been thinking about opening a railroad museum here in town.
(C) He is even thinking about opening a railroad museum here in town.
(D) He started to think about opening a railroad museum here in town.
(E) He once had even been thinking about opening a railroad museum here in town.

DAILY SPARK ENGLISH TEST PREP

Sentence Completions

Complete the sentences by choosing the best answers.

The _____ celebrated by the bar, completely oblivious to the fact that his girlfriend was sitting in the corner with a _____ look on her face.

(A) patron . . . gleeful
(B) benefactor . . . jovial
(C) reveler . . . sour
(D) patriarch . . . disjointed
(E) candidate . . . victorious

Three foreign governments have been searching for him for nearly a decade, but the spy has proved to be _____ and _____.

(A) revered . . . forlorn
(B) indistinct . . . conspicuous
(C) stealthy . . . elusive
(D) abominable . . . retractable
(E) indestructible . . . fragile

Read the passage and choose the best answers to the questions that follow it.

(1) The agency makes an annual report to the state government about the per capita consumption of water at both the state and local levels. (2) Water consumption includes drinking water, watering lawns, washing cars, running dishwashers, and anything else involving the use of water. (3) During the past calendar year, the state has received an above-average amount of rain, so the agency predicts that per capita water consumption will be slightly below normal. (4) The agency's annual report should be available to the public late in the first quarter.

Which of the following statements is implied by the passage above?
(A) Consumers use more water when it rains more.
(B) An increase in rain may cause a decrease in water consumption.
(C) Fewer consumers use water for drinking during the rainy season.
(D) An increase in rainfall may deplete the water reserves.
(E) The agency waits until after the rainy season to publish its reports.

"Per capita" means
(A) everyone
(B) population
(C) per person
(D) per state
(E) average

Choose the answer that most improves the <u>underlined portion</u> of the original sentence. If the original sentence does not have an error, choose (A).

The fanciest restaurants in the city <u>require its</u> male patrons to wear suit jackets.
(A) require its
(B) requires its
(C) require their
(D) requires their
(E) requires of their

Noah purchased <u>neither the coffee nor the hot cocoa.</u>
(A) neither the coffee nor the hot cocoa
(B) not the coffee nor the hot cocoa
(C) neither the coffee or the hot cocoa
(D) either the coffee but the hot cocoa
(E) either the coffee nor the hot cocoa

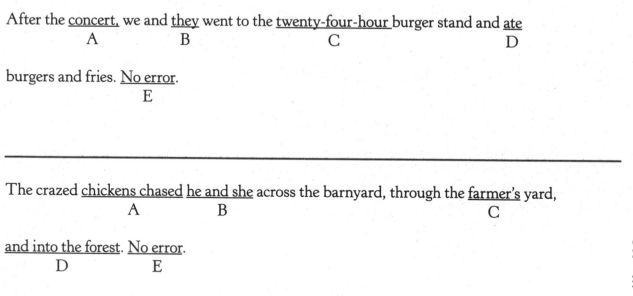

Identifying Sentence Errors

If there is an error, choose the <u>one underlined part</u> that must be changed to make the sentence correct. If there is no error, choose (E).

After the <u>concert,</u> we and <u>they</u> went to the <u>twenty-four-hour</u> burger stand and <u>ate</u>
        A   B   C   D

burgers and fries. <u>No error</u>.
          E

The crazed <u>chickens chased</u> <u>he and she</u> across the barnyard, through the <u>farmer's</u> yard,
          A   B   C

<u>and into the forest</u>. <u>No error</u>.
      D   E

DAILY SPARK ENGLISH TEST PREP

© 2004 SparkNotes LLC

Choose the answer that most improves the <u>underlined portion</u> of the original sentence. If the original sentence does not have an error, choose (A).

Regardless of what she says, I'm more likely to get elected <u>than her</u>.

(A) than her
(B) than she
(C) than she saw
(D) than she had seen
(E) than she have

Of all the thousands of species of fish beneath the sea, the most ferocious <u>one of them all are</u> the barracuda.

(A) one of them all are
(B) ones of them all is
(C) ones of them all are
(D) is
(E) are

Read the passage and choose the best answers to the questions that follow it.

(1) Several fringe economists recently published a paper in which they argue that credit has been the undoing of the American economy. (2) The government has put the economy in jeopardy by exceeding its credit limit; families live beyond their means and run up huge credit card debt. (3) In order to reverse this trend, the economists recommend the abolition of all credit in America and nationwide amnesty for all credit debt. (4) They advocate a cash-only economy, in which those people who want to make a big purchase will have to wait until they have enough cash to do so.

With which of the following statements would the economists most likely agree?
(A) Using credit responsibly is the way to avoid financial hardship.
(B) The government uses credit more wisely than does the average consumer.
(C) A cash-only economy would benefit everyone except those who make minimum wage.
(D) In addition to receiving amnesty from credit debt, consumers should receive amnesty from the fines and fees they owe to libraries, courts, etc.
(E) Families paying off car loans and home mortgages often abuse their credit cards.

Which of the following can be inferred from the passage?
(A) The government may be interested in considering the economists' proposal.
(B) The author has been persuaded by the economists' paper.
(C) The author sees many strengths in the economists' theory.
(D) The author does not think highly of the economists' paper.
(E) Bankers may be interested in the economists' plan.

Read the passage and choose the best answer to the question that follows it.

(1) Researchers and women have long known that many men are fixated on gadgets and electric gizmos. (2) The remote control, in particular, exercises a hypnotic effect on men. (3) Even men who aren't watching any particular show on television still want to have the remote and be in charge of changing channels. (4) Researchers are trying to determine if men have a fixation with the remote or if they just want control over the TV. (5) Women everywhere will be anxiously awaiting the results of the researchers studies.

In the context of the paragraph, which of the following revisions does sentence 5 most need?
(A) Replace "will be" with "were."
(B) Replace "researchers" with "researcher's."
(C) Replace "researchers" with "researchers'."
(D) Add a comma after "awaiting."
(E) Replace "awaiting" with "waiting."

Sentence Completions

Complete the sentences by choosing the best answers.

The _____ daughter did not inherit her mother's _____ for saving money.
(A) prodigal . . . enthusiasm
(B) miserly . . . tenacity
(C) parsimonious . . . affliction
(D) ineluctable . . . paradigm
(E) zealous . . . prerequisite

During the blackout, scared children had to be _____ from trapped elevators.
(A) extricated
(B) indicated
(C) inundated
(D) truncated
(E) disgruntled

© 2004 SparkNotes LLC

Read the passage and choose the best answers to the questions that follow it.

(1) In recent years, the sheer volume of students applying to college has led application committees to rely on standardized test scores, which they say indicate a student's likeliness to succeed in college. (2) College admissions tests are not the only standardized test that students take, however. (3) The Advanced Placement exams are another kind of standardized test taken by thousands of students every year. (4) The U.S. armed forces give a standardized test called the ASVAB to identify potential candidates for entry into the military. (5) Because of this institutional emphasis on standardized tests, the federal government should step in and design a national high school curriculum. (6) This would allow school districts to measure the performance of their students against national standards. (7) It would also help prepare students to excel on standardized tests.

The passage implies that which of the following would be one benefit of a national high school curriculum?
(A) the potential to earn college credit in high school
(B) the potential for early acceptance into the military
(C) the increased likelihood that students will excel in college
(D) good preparation for a rigorous college curriculum
(E) good preparation for standardized tests

The author expresses what kind of feelings about a national curriculum?
(A) bewilderment
(B) objectivity
(C) contempt
(D) enthusiasm
(E) nostalgia

Choose the answer that most improves the <u>underlined portion</u> of the original sentence. If the original sentence does not have an error, choose (A).

No matter how hard she looks, Jeannie <u>can't never find</u> four-leaf clovers in her backyard.
(A) can't never find
(B) can never find
(C) never can't find
(D) never can find
(E) never can't find

A loud voice spoke over the intercom, giving the students <u>instructions for the fire drill; quietly exit the classroom, move down the stairs, and congregate near the back of the parking lot</u>.
(A) instructions for the fire drill; quietly exit the classroom, move down the stairs, and congregate near the back of the parking lot
(B) instructions for the fire drill: quietly exit the classroom move down the stairs and congregate near the back of the parking lot
(C) instructions for the fire drill: quietly exit the classroom, move down the stairs, and congregate near the back of the parking lot
(D) instructions: for the fire drill, quietly exit the classroom, move down the stairs and congregate near the back of the parking lot
(E) instructions for the fire drill, quietly exit the classroom, move down the stairs, and congregate near the back of the parking lot

If there is an error, choose the <u>one underlined part</u> that must be changed to make the sentence correct. If there is no error, choose (E).

<u>Its</u> incredible <u>to think</u> that just a few short years ago, the site of the shopping mall complex
A   B

<u>was</u> no more than a <u>pasture full</u> of cows and horses. <u>No error</u>.
C   D   E

Bobby waited at the train station all <u>afternoon</u> just <u>hoping to catch</u> a glance of the
A   B

<u>celebrities they</u> were taking the train as part of a promotional event the train company
C

<u>was sponsoring</u>. <u>No error</u>.
D   E

Choose the answer that most improves the <u>underlined portion</u> of the original sentence. If the original sentence does not have an error, choose (A).

At the bottom of the <u>canyon winds a dusty path that is over a mile deep</u>.
(A) canyon winds a dusty path that is over a mile deep
(B) canyon, which winds a dusty path, is over a mile deep
(C) canyon, winds a dusty path, that is over a mile deep
(D) canyon, winds a dusty path that, is over a mile deep
(E) canyon, which is over a mile deep, winds a dusty path

The most relaxing music, at least in my dentist's opinion, <u>are those that feature</u> both piano and saxophone.
(A) are those that feature
(B) are those who feature
(C) are those which feature
(D) is that that features
(E) features

Read the passage and choose the best answer to the question that follows it.

(1) The issue of cloning has stirred up emotions in the scientific world, the religious world, the academic world, and even in the agricultural world. (2) Most people don't mind the cloning of grains and other vegetation, but some are uneasy about the cloning of such animals as mice, rats, and sheep. (3) What really upsets people is the idea of cloning a human. (4) Human cloning would greatly advance our knowledge of genetics, cancer research, and other areas of science and medicine, but religious leaders and human rights activists raise moral questions about the practice.

Based on the information in the passage, which of the following clones would cause the least amount of controversy?
(A) a rabbit
(B) a cow
(C) a chicken
(D) a potato plant
(E) a monkey

If there is an error, choose the <u>one underlined part</u> that must be changed to make the sentence correct. If there is no error, choose (E).

We <u>thumbed</u> <u>threw</u> the articles in the sports section of the newspaper <u>but we</u> could not
    A   B   C

find any coverage of the junior varsity volleyball tournament <u>that was held</u> at our school
                                                     D

over the weekend. <u>No error</u>.
                 E

Autograph seekers followed the celebrities and <u>ask</u> them for <u>their signatures</u> on items
                                 A   B

<u>such as photos</u>, albums, T-shirts, and even on body parts, such as <u>arms and foreheads</u>.
   C

<u>No error</u>.
  E

Read the passage and choose the best answers to the questions that follow it.

(1) The instructor entered the room in a pompous manner and introduced himself as if he were some kind of celebrity. (2) He looked out across the sea of students and let out a sigh. (3) Reluctantly, he opened his notes and launched into an introductory lesson on macroeconomics. (4) After just a few minutes, the instructor looked at the students, shrugged his shoulders, and slammed his notebook shut. (5) Then he turned up his nose and strolled out of the lecture hall.

In sentence 1, the word "pompous" means
(A) confused
(B) uncomfortable
(C) arrogant
(D) bored
(E) concerned

Based on the passage above, which of the following is the most likely conclusion?
(A) There were no students in the lecture hall.
(B) The students didn't like the instructor.
(C) The instructor was in the wrong lecture hall.
(D) The instructor didn't feel like teaching these students.
(E) The instructor was late for a meeting.

Read the passage and choose the best answer to the question that follows it.

(1) The legal limit for one's blood alcohol level while driving is 0.08. (2) Most people don't realize that they reach this limit after as few as one or two drinks. (3) Perhaps if portable breath tests were made readily available; more people would become aware of their own alcohol tolerance level. (4) This, in turn, would lead to less drunken driving. (5) It remains to be seen, however, whether portable breath tests would lead to fewer alcohol-related accidents.

In the context of the paragraph, which of the following is the best revision of sentence 3?

(A) Perhaps if portable breath tests were made readily available, more people would become aware of their own alcohol tolerance level.

(B) Perhaps if portable breath tests were made readily available: more people would become aware of their own alcohol tolerance level.

(C) Perhaps if portable breath tests were made readily available. More people would become aware of their own alcohol tolerance level.

(D) Perhaps if portable breath tests were made readily available, and more people would become aware of their own alcohol tolerance level.

(E) Perhaps, if portable breath tests were made readily available; more people might just become aware of their own alcohol tolerance level.

79

If there is an error, choose the <u>one underlined part</u> that must be changed to make the sentence correct. If there is no error, choose (E).

Some of Becky's favorite movie stars <u>begin</u> <u>their</u> <u>careers</u> many years ago on <u>television, specifically</u>
                                      A   B   C   D

on soap operas. <u>No error</u>.
                E

As the helicopter <u>hovers</u> over the <u>volcano,</u> the scientist leaned out the door <u>and filmed</u> the
                     A   B   C

<u>fiery, molten</u> lava below. <u>No error</u>.
    D   E

Read the passage and choose the best answers to the questions that follow it.

(1) Thousands of years ago, the ancient Hebrews constructed a box called the Ark of the Covenant, in which they kept some of their most precious relics. (2) Eventually, the king of Israel constructed a temple for the ark. (3) At some point in history, the ark disappeared. (4) Some historians believe it was moved to Elephantine Island; others believe the Babylonians looted the Temple of Solomon and took the ark. (5) Still others believe the ark is hidden in a chapel in Ethiopia. (6) Many archaeologists have devoted their lives to finding the ark; Harrison Ford starred in a movie inspired by their quest.

Which of the following conclusions can be made based on the passage?
(A) Scientists know where the Ark of the Covenant was in 400 B.C.E.
(B) Historians have one primary theory as to the whereabouts of the Ark of the Covenant.
(C) The exact location of the ark has yet to be determined.
(D) The Ark of the Covenant is the most sacred of all religious artifacts.
(E) We will never know the exact location of the Ark of the Covenant.

In sentence 1 of the first paragraph, the word "relics" means
(A) old items
(B) antique items
(C) ancient items
(D) items of religious significance
(E) items of scientific importance

Sentence Completions

Complete the sentences by choosing the best answers.

The mule, which was either _____ or just plain _____, refused to budge once we'd reached the bottom of the valley.
(A) sophomoric . . . excited
(B) contrite . . . belligerent
(C) lethargic . . . obstinate
(D) contrary . . . cooperative
(E) pugnacious . . . accommodating

Marvin, the quintessential _____, gave away nearly his entire _____.
(A) philanthropist . . . inheritance
(B) strategist . . . portfolio
(C) cynic . . . plan
(D) miser . . . fortune
(E) malingerer . . . estate

Choose the answer that most improves the <u>underlined portion</u> of the original sentence. If the original sentence does not have an error, choose (A).

Hundreds of years ago, sailors feared <u>they</u> might fall off the edge of the world.
(A) they
(B) them
(C) sailing vessels
(D) the mermaids
(E) sailors, mariners, and mermaids

If a genie can grant only three wishes to someone, why can't <u>they</u> just use the third wish to ask for three more wishes?
(A) they
(B) them
(C) the genie
(D) the wisher
(E) he

Read the passage and choose the best answers to the questions that follow it.

(1) In recent years, school boards across the country have slashed budgets in attempts to balance the books and make up for federal funding cuts. (2) More often than not, music programs are the first programs to get cut. (3) Instruments, sheet music, music instructors, and concerts are expensive, and music programs typically generate very little revenue. (4) These factors often put music programs at risk when it comes time to trim the budget. (5) Most schools wouldn't dream of cutting their football programs, even though music provides many more tangible benefits to many more students than does football.

According to the author, most school boards decide which programs to cut based on which factor?
(A) student enrollment in the programs
(B) alumni attendance at program exhibitions and competitions
(C) program performance during competitions
(D) student preference
(E) revenue generated by the programs

The author of the passage seems to be
(A) biased against music programs
(B) partial to music programs
(C) biased against rock bands
(D) partial to school board members
(E) partial to athletic programs in general

Complete the sentences by choosing the best answers.

Councilman Moscowitz supports the construction of a park not for its ecological value, but for its _____ value.
(A) intrinsic
(B) aesthetic
(C) prolific
(D) diametric
(E) systolic

Jack is _____ about his own appearance, but he is _____ about his apartment, which he cleans almost every day.
(A) harmonious . . . muddled
(B) conflicted . . . luxurious
(C) incongruent . . . ornamental
(D) affluent . . . meager
(E) lackadaisical . . . fastidious

Identifying Sentence Errors

If there is an error, choose the <u>one underlined part</u> that must be changed to make the sentence correct. If there is no error, choose (E).

<u>Despite the warnings</u> printed on the <u>label,</u> the customer <u>guzzled</u> the coffee and burned
        A   B   C

<u>her tongue</u>. <u>No error</u>.
   D   E

<u>Clarissa, a hopeless romantic,</u> felt her heart flutter <u>when David opened</u> the door <u>for her</u>
        A   B   C

<u>at the restaurant</u>. <u>No error</u>.
   D   E

Read the passage and choose the best answers to the questions that follow it.

(1) Many children believe that monsters hide in their closets and under their beds, waiting to attack them during the night. (2) Children scared of monsters often call to their parents. (3) Many parents, faced with their frightened child, go to the closet or bend down to the floor and command the "monsters" to leave their children alone. (4) Imagine the surprise of the child when his parent confirms that indeed there are monsters lurking about. (5) Parents may think they are being cute or assuaging their child's fears when they pretend to banish the monsters, but what they're really doing is worsening the fear. (6) Experts say that in this situation, parents should assure their children that monsters don't exist.

One can infer from the passage that children want their parents to
(A) threaten the monsters
(B) politely ask the monsters to leave the premises
(C) assure them that monsters have not been seen for thousands of years
(D) assure them that monsters do not exist
(E) assure them that the monsters are gone for now

In sentence 5, the word "assuaging" means
(A) dismissing
(B) admitting
(C) prohibiting
(D) discouraging
(E) lessening

86

Identifying Sentence Errors

If there is an error, choose the <u>one underlined part</u> that must be changed to make the sentence correct. If there is no error, choose (E).

The spokeswoman for City Hall <u>scheduled</u> a press conference for <u>today—a</u> press
                                  A   B

conference <u>at that</u> she's going to make a big <u>announcement</u>. <u>No error</u>.
            C   D   E

After six months <u>in the city,</u> the country bumpkin <u>had</u> difficulty <u>readjusting</u> to things like
                  A   B   C

bugs, dirt, and roosters <u>crowing</u> at dawn. <u>No error</u>.
                                D   E

Choose the answer that most improves the <u>underlined portion</u> of the original sentence. If the original sentence does not have an error, choose (A).

He took guitar lessons from <u>an instructor who has</u> an advanced degree in music.

(A) an instructor who has
(B) an instructor; he has
(C) an instructor, who has
(D) an instructor that has
(E) an instructor: he has

Although candles create a romantic atmosphere and sometimes a pleasant aroma, <u>it also can be</u> a fire hazard if left unattended.

(A) it also can be
(B) it also could be
(C) but also can be
(D) they also can be
(E) also can be

88

Read the passage and choose the best answers to the questions that follow it.

(1) Only a little over a century ago, photographers were taking grainy black-and-white photos of poor quality. (2) Today, though, with digital technology advancing and progressing every day. (3) The quality of photography has reached levels never before imagined. (4) The clarity and vividness of today's pictures had far exceeded anything available even a few years ago.

Which of the following revisions does sentence 2 most need?
(A) Add an apostrophe to "today."
(B) Replace "every day" with "everyday."
(C) Replace "every" with "each."
(D) Replace "advancing and progressing" with "advanced and progressed."
(E) Combine sentence 2 with sentence 3.

Which of the following revisions does sentence 4 most need?
(A) Remove the word "had."
(B) Replace "had" with "has."
(C) Replace "had" with "have."
(D) Replace "exceeded" with "excepted."
(E) Replace "ever" with "never."

Read the passage and choose the best answers to the questions that follow it.

(1) State College recently passed a liberal and experimental new policy under which professors are not required to check attendance during the semester. (2) Under the provisions of the new policy, students will be graded solely on the basis of assignments and exams. (3) Proponents of the new policy argue that doing away with attendance will lessen professors' paperwork and save valuable time in class. (4) Opponents of the policy worry that students will attend class only when assignments are due or when exams are scheduled. (5) Most students, when interviewed, thought attendance wouldn't be greatly affected by the new policy.

Which of the following statements best sums up the new policy?
(A) Professors are no longer required to attend class on a regular basis.
(B) Assignments and exams may be turned in at any point during the semester.
(C) Students are no longer required to attend class in order to pass a course.
(D) Students are only required to attend classes at which professors will announce important dates or information.
(E) The Board of Regents approved the new policy.

Which of the following could be inferred from the passage?
(A) In the past, professors have been very strict about attendance.
(B) In the past, the college has insisted on impeccable attendance records.
(C) Students have long pushed for a more relaxed academic environment.
(D) Students have long been stifled by restrictive attendance policies.
(E) Students have not been particularly angered by stringent attendance requirements.

Identifying Sentence Errors

If there is an error, choose the <u>one underlined part</u> that must be changed to make the sentence correct. If there is no error, choose (E).

The craftsman, who <u>had been</u> making watches for nearly forty years, <u>retires</u> from the
               A   B

business last month to spend his final days traveling the world and experiencing other
                     C   D

cultures. <u>No error</u>.
        E

I <u>have always been</u> afraid to <u>have gone</u> into the haunted house that the local high school
    A   B

<u>builds</u> every <u>year, because I get</u> really nervous in close quarters. <u>No error</u>.
 C   D   E

Read the passage and choose the best answers to the questions that follow it.

(1) For months, the company of soldiers had been training all day and tossing and turning all night. (2) Now, the day they had been waiting for was finally upon them. (3) Drumbeats in the distance brought the men to attention; they stopped performing their morning chores. (4) After a moment of hesitation, the soldiers hurried to gather their supplies and belongings. (5) They put out the campfires and lined up in formation. (6) With the drumbeats still echoing through the campsite, the soldiers began to march in a cadence of their own. (7) With every step, their dread mounted.

On "the day they had been waiting for," what will occur?
(A) demobilizing
(B) evacuation
(C) battle
(D) marching practice
(E) surrender

"Cadence," from sentence 6, means
(A) a rhyme
(B) a rhythm
(C) a dance
(D) a melody
(E) a harmony

Read the passage and choose the best answers to the questions that follow it.

(1) Experts recommend that parents wash their infants once a week. (2) If they are washed more frequently, their skin can get dried out and chapped. (3) Many older mothers and grandmothers dispute this recommendation and say that babies can be washed every day just like anyone else. (4) Regardless of these competing theories, babies don't like water in their eyes.

Which of the following is the best revision of sentence 2?
(A) If infants are washed more frequently, their skin can get dried out and chapped
(B) If they are washed more frequently, skin has get dried out and chapped.
(C) If infants are washed more frequently: their skin can get dried out and.
(D) If they are washed more frequently their skin can get dried out; and chapped.
(E) If infants are washed more frequently, they're skin can get dried out and chapped.

In the context of the paragraph, which of the following is the best revision of sentence 4?
(A) Regardless of these competing theories, babies don't like water in their eyes.
(B) Regardless of these competing theories, everyone agrees that babies don't like getting water in their eyes.
(C) Regardless of which advice is correct, babies don't like water in their eyes, regardless.
(D) Regardless, neither piece of advice is correct, babies don't like water in their eyes.
(E) Regardless of whether or not the advice is correct, babies don't like water in their eyes according to experts and mothers and grandmothers alike.

Complete the sentences by choosing the best answers.

The _____ sailor risked his life to save the passengers aboard the sinking ship.
(A) intrepid
(B) insipid
(C) indecisive
(D) inclusive
(E) inductive

The mighty _____ was _____ to attack, standing firm even under the heaviest sieges.
(A) fortress . . . impervious
(B) bulwark . . . vulnerable
(C) encampment . . . doomed
(D) citadel . . . feasible
(E) bastion . . . credible

© 2004 SparkNotes LLC

Read the passage and choose the best answers to the questions that follow it.

(1) When food companies advertise their products on TV, viewers are more likely to buy those products on their next visit to the grocery store. (2) Advertisers especially like to promote food items during sporting events, even though networks charge steeply for this kind of airtime. (3) Market research shows that ads that run during sporting events have a higher rate of success than those same ads run at different times and during different shows.

Which of the following works best as the final sentence of the paragraph?
(A) Even though running TV ads is expensive, most food companies argue that it's money well spent.
(B) Advertising executives milk the food industry for as much money as possible.
(C) Television networks make most of their money from food advertisers.
(D) Television networks make most of their money from ads run during sporting events.
(E) Print ads are another matter.

Based on the passage, which of the following is most likely to be true?
(A) TV ads for food rarely show people eating.
(B) Food companies prefer advertising on TV to advertising on radio.
(C) Sports fans tend to be heavy.
(D) People shown eating in TV ads are often real consumers.
(E) Marketing executives cater to food advertisers.

Choose the answer that most improves the <u>underlined portion</u> of the original sentence. If the original sentence does not have an error, choose (A).

<u>Kneepads, elbow pads, and a helmet is required</u> at the skate park.
(A) Kneepads, elbow pads, and a helmet is required
(B) Kneepads, elbow pads, and, a helmet, is required
(C) Kneepads, elbow pads, and a helmet requires
(D) Kneepads, elbow pads, and a helmet are required
(E) Kneepads, elbow pads, and a helmet, is required

The fashion experts, according to the report on the news last night, <u>has declared</u> leopard prints officially out of style.
(A) has declared
(B) hasn't declared
(C) have declared
(D) has yet to declare
(E) declares

Identifying Sentence Errors

If there is an error, choose the <u>one underlined part</u> that must be changed to make the sentence correct. If there is no error, choose (E).

The cruise ship captain announced <u>over the loudspeaker</u> that the buffet <u>would include</u> roast beef,
                                             A   B

rolls, and salad, and that the dance party <u>would follow</u> dinner <u>and features disco music</u>. <u>No error</u>.
                                             C   D   E

<u>Every year</u> the teachers at the academy <u>goes</u> to the museum <u>to admire</u> the work of the
A   B   C

greatest artists <u>of the last five hundred years</u>. <u>No error</u>.
                          D   E

Read the passage and choose the best answer to the question that follows it.

(1) Educational research and testing experts say that the place where a student studies should be quiet and comfortable—but not so quiet and comfortable that the studier is tempted to fall asleep. (2) Typically, students study while sitting on a bed. (3) Many students listen to the radio or watch television while studying. (4) Testing experts would frown on all of these habits, but that's not going to stop students from practicing them anytime soon.

Which of the following is the main idea of the paragraph?
(A) Students should avoid falling asleep while studying.
(B) Radio and television actually aid study, despite what experts say.
(C) Students usually ignore educational experts.
(D) Although experts recommend a particular study environment, students often have their own study habits.
(E) Studying presents an interesting dilemma for students who like radio and television.

DAILY SPARK ENGLISH TEST PREP

Choose the answer that most improves the <u>underlined portion</u> of the original sentence. If the original sentence does not have an error, choose (A).

Inevitably, right after I wash my car, it rains <u>and gets dirty all over again</u>.
(A) and gets dirty all over again
(B) my car then gets dirty all over again
(C) and my car gets dirty all over again
(D) and gets dirty once again
(E) and, my car gets dirty all over again

As the sun came up, <u>the sailors filed off the ship one by one and began to search for his family</u>.
(A) the sailors filed off the ship one by one and began to search for his family
(B) the sailors filed off the ship one by one and began his search for his family
(C) the sailor filed off the ship one by one and began his search for his family
(D) the sailors filed off the ship one by one and began to search for their family
(E) the sailors filed off the ship one by one and began to search for their families

DAILY SPARK ENGLISH TEST PREP

Read the passage and choose the best answer to the question that follows it.

(1) Research has shown that infants prefer bright colors besides subdued hues. (2) This is because infants have difficulty seeing lighter shades. (3) Interestingly, subtle shades continue to be more popular than bright colors in infant nursery room themes. (4) This shows that nurseries are more often decorated with the taste of the parents, rather than the infant, in mind. (5) Tradition also plays a role; many parents have always associated pastels with children. (6) Luckily, most infant toys are brightly colored.

Which revision does sentence 1 most need?
(A) Replace "has" with "have."
(B) Replace "that" with "those."
(C) Add a comma after "shown."
(D) Replace "besides" with "to"
(E) Replace "besides" with "than."

Read the passage and choose the best answer to the question that follows it.

(1) Moral education is the training of the heart and mind toward good. (2) In his *Book of Virtues*, William Bennett suggests that there is nothing more influential in a child's life than the moral power of quiet example. (3) For children to take moral responsibility seriously, he claims, they must grow up around adults who do so. (4) In other words, children do what they see, not what they are told.

Based on the passage above, it can be inferred that the author believes
(A) that children learn from both books and from teachers
(B) that children might be influenced more by teachers than by other role models
(C) that children must be told about morals repeatedly before they sink in
(D) that role models may be more important in the development of children than lessons learned from books
(E) that morals, among other things, must be read about rather than witnessed

101

If there is an error, choose the <u>one underlined part</u> that must be changed to make the sentence correct. If there is no error, choose (E).

If you <u>have</u> a few minutes after <u>work, please</u> swing by the market and <u>pick</u> up the
    A   B   C

following <u>items,</u> milk, eggs, bread, mustard, napkins, and bananas. <u>No error</u>.
          D   E

The most beloved poet of the last few decades <u>lives</u> just down the street from another
                                              A

celebrated writer, <u>one who</u> <u>had happened</u> to be the most <u>celebrated</u> essayist of the last
                      B   C   D

few decades. <u>No error</u>.
           E

Complete the sentences by choosing the best answers.

The Garcias wanted a dog that was neither hyper and quick to bark nor so _____ that it never moved from the couch.
(A) rambunctious
(B) lethargic
(C) defenseless
(D) insipid
(E) demeaning

Jane hoped to _____ her students' misbehavior by promising them cookies if they shaped up.
(A) enlist
(B) provoke
(C) invoke
(D) evoke
(E) curtail

Read the passage and choose the best answers to the questions that follow it.

(1) Becky wanted to supplement her income, so she decided to buy items at garage sales and then sell them in an online auction. (2) She woke up early on Saturday morning and traveled around the city, stopping at nearly two dozen garage sales. (3) She spent $250 at the sales. (4) After spending just a few hours setting up the auctions online, Becky sat back and watched. (5) When the auctions concluded three days later, Becky had sold all of her items for a total of $1,565.

In sentence 1, the word "supplement" means
(A) distribute
(B) increase threefold
(C) create
(D) decrease
(E) add to

Which of the following conclusions can be made based on the information in the passage?
(A) Becky was out of work before she started her online business.
(B) Becky made more from her auctions than she did from her other job.
(C) Becky is a poor businesswoman.
(D) Becky made back all the money she invested.
(E) Becky's auctions were a bust.

© 2004 SparkNotes LLC

If there is an error, choose the <u>one underlined part</u> that must be changed to make the sentence correct. If there is no error, choose (E).

Sometimes <u>it seems</u> that everyone in America <u>has</u> a cell phone <u>except for</u> I. <u>No error</u>.
          A   B   C   D   E

The models parading <u>back and forth</u> across the runway never <u>looking</u> down at the
                   A   B

audience <u>but rather gaze</u> out <u>above the heads</u> of everyone watching. <u>No error</u>.
          C   D   E

Choose the answer that most improves the <u>underlined portion</u> of the original sentence. If the original sentence does not have an error, choose (A).

The feature story was read by thousands of interested citizens.
(A) The feature story was read by thousands of interested citizens.
(B) The feature story got read by thousands of interested citizens.
(C) The feature story had gotten read by thousands of interested citizens.
(D) The feature story were read by thousands of interested citizens.
(E) Thousands of interested citizens read the feature story.

At the junior high school dance, the boys stood on one side of the <u>room and</u> the girls stood on the other.
(A) room and
(B) room, and
(C) room,
(D) room; and
(E) room;

Reading Comprehension

Read the passage and choose the best answers to the questions that follow it.

(1) On March 4, 1865, with the end of the Civil War in sight, President Abraham Lincoln delivered his second inaugural address. (2) An excerpt from that speech:

> With malice toward none, with charity for all, with firmness in the right as God gives us to see the right, let us strive on to finish the work we are in, to bind up the nation's wounds, to care for him who shall have borne the battle and for his widow and his orphan, to do all which may achieve and cherish a just and lasting peace among ourselves and with all nations.

The term "inaugural address" in sentence 1 means
(A) a letter written to an inaugural committee
(B) a speech given when being sworn in
(C) a debate with another candidate
(D) a speech given while campaigning
(E) an article written for a government publication

In the first sentence of the inaugural address, the phrase "the work we are in" most likely refers to which of the following?
(A) a campaign for the presidency
(B) a campaign for the House of Representatives
(C) the Civil War
(D) Reconstruction
(E) writing an inaugural address

Read the passage and choose the best answer to the question that follows it.

(1) Economists estimate that consumers spent nearly $4 billion last year on online auctions. (2) Consumer advocates contend that the government has no right to collect taxes on such purchases. (3) They maintain that consumers will greatly reduce the number of purchases they make online if taxes are imposed politicians who support online taxes argue that the sales of items online will not be affected.

Which of the following is the best revision of sentence 3?

(A) They maintain that consumers will greatly reduce the number of purchases they make online if taxes are imposed. In conclusion, politicians who support online taxes argue that the sales of items online will not be affected.

(B) They maintain that consumers will greatly reduce the number of purchases they make online if taxes are imposed, therefore, politicians who support online taxes argue that the sales of items online will not be affected.

(C) They maintain that consumers will greatly reduce the number of purchases they make online if taxes are imposed. Politicians, who support online taxes argue that the sales of items online, will not be affected.

(D) They maintain that consumers will greatly reduce the number of purchases they make online if taxes are imposed. Politicians who support online taxes argue that the sales of items online will not be affected.

(E) They maintain that consumers will greatly reduce the number of purchases they make online if taxes are imposed by politicians who support online taxes argue that the sales of items online will not be affected.

Complete the sentences by choosing the best answers.

Most of the teachers thought Jill was _____, but Coach Rogers never gave up on her, and as a result, she was totally _____ by graduation.

(A) reputable . . . discouraged
(B) incorrigible . . . transformed
(C) introverted . . . intrinsic
(D) malleable . . . stubborn
(E) harmless . . . detrimental

Amy drank bottle after bottle of water, but her thirst was _____.

(A) indestructible
(B) insatiable
(C) invective
(D) infectious
(E) inflammatory

Read the passage and choose the best answer to the question that follows it.

(1) A year ago, the majority of the workers at BigMoneyCorp commuted to work every day. (2) A company study showed that the average worker spent one hour and twenty minutes traveling from the suburbs of Atlanta to the city. (3) In response, the CEO moved the headquarters to the suburbs. (4) In the year since the move, BigMoneyCorp's profit margins have improved. (5) Furthermore, company employees have requested fewer sick days and personal days in the one year since the move than they had in the five years prior to the move.

Based on the passage above, what factors might be responsible for the increased productivity at BigMoneyCorp?
(A) state-of-the-art facilities at the new location
(B) reduced stress for employees
(C) sense of community among commuters
(D) the economy
(E) an improved CEO

If there is an error, choose the <u>one underlined part</u> that must be changed to make the sentence correct. If there is no error, choose (E).

On <u>our field trip</u> last week, <u>we went</u> <u>not</u> only to the art museum <u>but plus</u> to the
   A   B   C   D

science and history museums. <u>No error</u>.
                          E

The cell phone manufacturer <u>hire</u> approximately two thousand new employees <u>every month</u>;
                           A   B

the manufacturer must <u>produce</u> more phones to compete in <u>today's market</u>. <u>No error</u>.
                   C   D   E

Complete the sentences by choosing the best answers.

The _____ pilot often ignored orders and criticized his commanders.
(A) clandestine
(B) maverick
(C) indolent
(D) unproductive
(E) fruitless

In an attempt to avoid media attention, the donor asked to remain _____.
(A) spontaneous
(B) spurious
(C) infamous
(D) notorious
(E) anonymous

DAILY SPARK ENGLISH TEST PREP

Choose the answer that most improves the <u>underlined portion</u> of the original sentence. If the original sentence does not have an error, choose (A).

The combination <u>of dirty socks and shoes shirts shorts sweatpants and practice jerseys</u> makes the locker room almost unbearably smelly.

(A) of dirty socks and shoes shirts shorts sweatpants and practice jerseys

(B) of: dirty socks and shoes shirts shorts sweatpants, and practice jerseys

(C) of dirty socks, shoes, shirts, shorts, sweatpants, and practice jerseys

(D) of: dirty socks, shoes, shirts, shorts, sweatpants, and practice jerseys

(E) of dirty socks and shoes and shirts and shorts and sweatpants and practice jerseys

As the fire engines raced down the street transporting firefighters and the fire chief, <u>they were very loud.</u>

(A) they were very loud

(B) they're very loud

(C) they are very loud

(D) the firefighters are very loud

(E) the sirens were very loud

Read the passage and choose the best answers to the questions that follow it.

(1) If sports build character, as conventional wisdom suggests, why do we always read about athletes getting arrested? (2) Some people cite the extravagant lifestyles of professional athletes; others suggest that years of special treatment make athletes believe that they are above the law. (3) Researchers at Baylor University's sport management department have another theory. (4) They have discovered that the percentage of professional athletes who get arrested is actually smaller than the percentage of doctors who get arrested. (5) Lawyers, teachers, and accountants also get arrested with greater frequency than do athletes. (6) This study suggests that the media frenzy that follows the arrest of an athlete causes the mistaken public perception that most athletes are criminals.

The study discussed in the passage indicates that
(A) stories of professionals being arrested always lead the news
(B) the media does nothing to enhance the image of professional athletes
(C) sports do not enhance character or develop integrity
(D) the media is inconsistent in its treatment of people who get arrested
(E) the police often target professional athletes

In sentence 6, the word "frenzy" means
(A) criticism
(B) attrition
(C) frequency
(D) uproar
(E) report

114

Read the passage and choose the best answer to the question that follows it.

(1) Many young boys dream of being firefighters when they grow up. (2) There are many things about the lives of firefighters that appeal to young boys. (3) Perhaps boys are fascinated with the big red fire engines. (4) Perhaps they like the idea of wearing big rubber boots. (5) Perhaps they like the idea of wearing a fire hat. (6) Maybe boys believe that fighting fires is exciting work. (7) It could also be that boys want to do heroic things and believe that being a firefighter is the way to be a hero.

Which of the following sentences is the best combination of sentences 4 and 5?
(A) Perhaps boys like the idea of wearing; big rubber boots, and a fire hat.
(B) Perhaps boys like the idea of wearing: big rubber boots and a fire hat.
(C) Perhaps a boy likes the ideas of wearing big rubber boots and a fire hat.
(D) Perhaps boys like the idea of wearing big rubber boots and a fire hat.
(E) Perhaps boys like the ideas of wearing big rubber boots and a fire hat.

Read the passage and choose the best answers to the questions that follow it.

(1) Archaeologists are scientists who study ancient cultures. (2) Archaeologists have been studying the ancient life and cultures of North America for many years. (3) Despite the years and years of research they've done, experts are still unable to determine when humans began living in America. (4) They do know, however, that by about 1000 B.C.E., farming villages had been established in eastern North America.

Which of the following conclusions can be made based on the passage?
(A) Without archaeologists, there would be no farming villages in North America.
(B) Without the work of archaeologists, we wouldn't know as much as we do about ancient life in North America.
(C) Farmers have been in North America for longer than archaeologists know.
(D) There is no evidence showing where people first lived in North America.
(E) An archaeologist is equal parts scientist, geologist, historian, anthropologist, and mathematician.

Which of the following is the main idea of the passage?
(A) Information provided by archaeologists is vital to understanding ancient life in North America.
(B) Information provided by archaeologists can also be used by anthropologists.
(C) We must learn more about ancient farmers in North America.
(D) Humans have not always lived in North America.
(E) Humans have not always farmed in North America.

Read the passage and choose the best answers to the questions that follow it.

(1) To answer the questions that have perplexed us through the ages—How was the world created? What causes weather? Why do seasons change? What happens after we die?—we have always turned to mythology. (2) Myths are stories that provide answers to otherwise unanswerable questions. (3) Thousands of years ago, stories we now study as literature were accepted as the truth about all the mysteries of nature and the universe. (4) Ancient man did not have the benefit of science and history, so ancient mythology should not strike us as unbelievable or far-fetched. (5) Moreover, many of our modern religious beliefs may be considered nothing more than mythology by future generations.

Which of the following statements can be inferred based on the passage?
(A) The strangest myths usually address the most puzzling existential questions.
(B) Myths that seem odd to us often make sense within the context of the culture that created them.
(C) Early myths are used to educate students in areas such as reading comprehension.
(D) Mythology should never be confused with religion.
(E) Mythology has never been satisfactorily disproved by modern religious thinkers.

In sentence 1, the word "perplexed" means
(A) mesmerized
(B) disenchanted
(C) condescended
(D) disgusted
(E) bewildered

If there is an error, choose the <u>one underlined part</u> that must be changed to make the sentence correct. If there is no error, choose (E).

After the fire department rescued the <u>family's</u> bird from the tree, the young boy <u>promised</u>
                                        A   B

he <u>wouldn't never</u> let the parakeet out of <u>its</u> cage again. <u>No error</u>.
    C   D   E

Advertisers <u>prefer</u> to do research before <u>they</u> buy television spots because they
        A   B

want <u>to know</u> <u>to which nights</u> their target audiences watch television. <u>No error</u>.
      C   D   E

Reading Comprehension

Read the passage and choose the best answers to the questions that follow it.

(1) Many people complain that major league baseball players make too much money. (2) Players' salaries, however, should be judged not against the average in other fields, but against the cream of the crop in other fields. (3) Major league players, the most talented men in their field, should be judged against the most talented businessmen, doctors, and lawyers, many of whom have immense yearly salaries. (4) People in the upper echelon of their field can expect to earn more than their less talented peers.

In sentence 4, the word "echelon" means
(A) distinction
(B) stratum
(C) consideration
(D) society
(E) room

The author of the passage displays which of the following attitudes toward major league baseball players and their salaries?
(A) cynical
(B) skeptical
(C) argumentative
(D) sympathetic
(E) synthetic

Choose the answer that most improves the <u>underlined portion</u> of the original sentence. If the original sentence does not have an error, choose (A).

The Science Foundation of America employees <u>researchers, which study all aspects of human behavior,</u> in order to advance knowledge.
(A) researchers, which study all aspects of human behavior,
(B) researchers, that study all aspects of human behavior,
(C) researchers, who study all aspects of human behavior,
(D) researchers, whom study all aspects of human behavior,
(E) researchers who study all aspects of human behavior

Advertisements claim that diet soda tastes exactly the same as regular <u>sodas; therefore, most diet sodas</u> taste distinctly of artificial sweeteners.
(A) sodas; therefore, most diet sodas
(B) sodas; however, most diet sodas
(C) sodas; although, most diet sodas
(D) sodas; and, most diet sodas
(E) sodas; though, most diet sodas

Reading Comprehension

Read the passage and choose the best answer to the question that follows it.

(1) Music videos have changed the way teenagers listen to music. (2) Thirty years ago, teens listened to music on the radio or on their eight-track tape players. (3) There were no visual images associated with the songs. (4) As a result, teens were free to interpret songs however they wanted. (5) Today, the music videos that accompany songs show interpretations of songs made by the artists and their producers. (6) When teens see the music videos, they have no choice but to associate songs with the images in the videos.

With which of the following statements would the author of this paragraph most likely agree?
(A) Music videos have enhanced songs for teens.
(B) Music videos have made today's songs more interesting for teens.
(C) Music videos have made it possible for teens to see the meanings behind songs that were formerly hidden.
(D) Music videos have reduced the ability of today's teens to interpret songs for themselves.
(E) Music videos are part of the natural evolution of the music industry.

Read the passage and choose the best answers to the questions that follow it.

(1) Learning to ride a bicycle without training wheels is not always a liberating experience. (2) The first time Marvin rode a bicycle without training wheels, he sped down the street and slammed into Mrs. Potter's tool shed. (3) Marvin escaped without bodily harm. (4) Marvin has no desire ever to get back on a bike. (5) Twenty years later, Marvin still can't bring himself to ride a bike. (6) Perhaps if his first experience with a two-wheel bike had ended different, Marvin might not have a phobia about bicycles.

Which of the following would be the best combination of sentence 3 and sentence 4?
(A) Marvin escaped without bodily harm and, therefore, Marvin has no desire to ever get back on a bike.
(B) Marvin escaped without bodily harm; Marvin has no desire ever to get back on a bike.
(C) Marvin escaped without bodily harm, but he has no desire ever to get back on a bike.
(D) Even though, Marvin, who had escaped without bodily harm, has no desire to get back, on a bike.
(E) Marvin has no desire to get back on a bike—he escaped without bodily harm.

Which of the following revisions does sentence 6 most need?
(A) Add "such things as" after "about."
(B) Replace "had ended" with "had not had ended."
(C) Add "been developed" after "have."
(D) Replace "two-wheel" with "two-wheeler-style."
(E) Replace "different" with "differently."

Complete the sentences by choosing the best answers.

King Charles was at the very _____ of his reign when the bicycle scandal broke, forcing him to _____.

(A) pinnacle . . . fluctuate
(B) nadir . . . venerate
(C) zenith . . . resign
(D) apex . . . alternate
(E) summit . . . disavow

Yolanda's many culinary disasters are too numerous to _____.

(A) confiscate
(B) incubate
(C) intonate
(D) enumerate
(E) elucidate

Read the passage and choose the best answers to the questions that follow it.

(1) Many children who love reading dream of writing books of their own one day. (2) For the most part, their dreams are dashed. (3) Publishers reject ninety-eight percent of all manuscript submissions. (4) For every book you see at your local bookstore, there are forty-nine other books out there that never got published. (5) The odds of becoming a published author are very slim.

(6) Despite the discouraging statistics, aspiring writers should take heart. (7) Some of the most successful authors swear that their best-selling works were rejected ten, fifteen, and even twenty times before a publisher finally took a chance on the manuscript. (8) These authors say that if a manuscript is good, it will get noticed eventually. (9) For those who dream of publishing and think they have the chops, established authors who faced down rejection should serve as inspirations.

Which of the following statements is true of the passage?
(A) The first paragraph is optimistic and the second paragraph is pessimistic.
(B) The first paragraph is pessimistic and the second paragraph is optimistic.
(C) The first paragraph is sarcastic.
(D) The second paragraph is jaded.
(E) Both paragraphs express the author's sarcasm.

In the passage, the word "manuscript" means
(A) book
(B) proposal
(C) definition
(D) poem
(E) letter

DAILY SPARK ENGLISH TEST PREP

If there is an error, choose the <u>one underlined part</u> that must be changed to make the sentence correct. If there is no error, choose (E).

Four Little League <u>teams advanced</u> to the state <u>tournament one</u> of them, the <u>team sponsored</u>
              A   B   C

by First State Bank, <u>is</u> from our hometown. <u>No error</u>.
                  D   E

<u>To aid</u> in the difficult task of <u>keeping track</u> of my car keys, I <u>attached</u> the keys to a big, metal key
 A   B   C

ring <u>which is approximately</u> the size of a CD. <u>No error</u>.
                D   E

Choose the answer that most improves the <u>underlined portion</u> of the original sentence. If the original sentence does not have an error, choose (A).

Children are usually the target audience for cereal <u>commercials, therefore, advertisers</u> often use animated characters in these commercials.
(A) commercials, therefore, advertisers
(B) commercials: therefore, advertisers
(C) commercials; therefore, advertisers
(D) commercials, therefore; advertisers
(E) commercials, therefore. Advertisers

Investors have suggested that diversifying one's portfolios <u>are the best way</u> to make money.
(A) are the best way
(B) are the best ways
(C) is the best way
(D) is the best ways
(E) is that way best

Reading Comprehension

Read the passage and choose the best answers to the questions that follow it.

(1) The city has made plans to close an area recreation center, pool, and playground. (2) They blame liability for the closure. (3) The Pleasant Valley Neighborhood Association opposes the closing and is planning a protest at City Hall. (4) The association has petitioned the city for an alternative recreation center of some kind, but the mayor's office has been unresponsive. (5) If the city continues with its plan to shut down the center, neighborhood parents would have to drive several miles to find a similar recreational facility. (6) However, many residents of the neighborhood are unable to do this for economic reasons.

Which of the following conclusions can be made based on the passage?
(A) The residents of Pleasant Valley live in the countryside.
(B) The residents of Pleasant Valley live in a very cold climate.
(C) The residents of Pleasant Valley are of a low socioeconomic status.
(D) The residents of Pleasant Valley have only recently organized the neighborhood association.
(E) The area recreation center is in a state of terrible disrepair.

In sentence 4, the phrase "has been unresponsive" means
(A) has been unable to respond
(B) has not offered a response
(C) has refused to correspond
(D) has responded in a confusing fashion
(E) has responded unnecessarily

Choose the answer that most improves the <u>underlined portion</u> of the original sentence. If the original sentence does not have an error, choose (A).

The neighbors' dogs barked all night long, and by morning we were furious <u>at them</u>.
(A) at them
(B) at the dogs
(C) because of them
(D) in spite of them
(E) with them

For two weeks, Tia and her boyfriend hiked through the <u>mountains; they were very tall</u>.
(A) mountains; they were very tall
(B) mountains; Tia and her boyfriend was very tall
(C) mountains, which were very tall
(D) mountains, hence they were very tall
(E) mountains: they were very tall

Read the passage and choose the best answers to the questions that follow it.

(1) In the middle of winter in places like North Dakota, temperatures commonly dip below zero degrees. (2) When temperatures drop to such extremes, activities slow to a crawl. (3) Cars won't start. (4) Snow covers roads and bridges. (5) Many businesses and workplaces stay closed because its workers can't get to work. (6) There really isn't much to do on such days rather than stay home, read a book, and try to stay warm.

Which of the following revisions does sentence 5 most need?
(A) Offset "and workplaces" with commas.
(B) Replace "stay closed" with "close."
(C) Replace "its" with "it's."
(D) Replace "its" with "their."
(E) Replace "its" with "they're."

Which of the following revisions does sentence 6 most need?
(A) Add a comma after "days."
(B) Replace "rather" with "other."
(C) Replace "than" with "then."
(D) Replace "There" with "Their."
(E) Add a colon after "days."

If there is an error, choose the <u>one underlined part</u> that must be changed to make the sentence correct. If there is no error, choose (E).

The entire fast-food industry <u>can trace</u> <u>it's</u> roots to the original fast-food hamburger
                                    A   B

restaurant <u>founded</u> nearly fifty years ago <u>by one man with a vision</u>. <u>No error</u>.
       C   D   E

Stunt men <u>put</u> their <u>life</u> on the line <u>every day</u> when they perform outrageous stunts,
         A   B   C

double for actors, and supervise explosions; their work <u>is</u> dangerous, but they love it. <u>No error</u>.
                                          D   E

Sentence Completions

Complete the sentences by choosing the best answers.

The president's vague, _____ remarks on the topic of gay marriage suggested that he himself was _____ about the issue.

(A) ambiguous . . . ambivalent

(B) zealous . . . articulate

(C) sincere . . . compassionate

(D) honest . . . forthcoming

(E) eloquent . . . inarticulate

We assumed the test would cover the most important concepts from our textbook, but, in fact, it covered _____ information.

(A) vital

(B) indispensable

(C) essential

(D) magnanimous

(E) trivial

Read the passage and choose the best answers to the questions that follow it.

(1) The teacher walked slowly to the teachers' lounge. (2) The class she had just finished had been a debacle. (3) She felt completely out of touch with the students. (4) Every pop culture event she'd referred to had drawn blank stares from the class. (5) When the students tried to talk about their own experiences, the teacher was baffled by their references. (6) She decided a little MTV–watching was in order.

In sentence 2, the word "debacle" means
(A) lesson
(B) quagmire
(C) catastrophe
(D) dissention
(E) conundrum

Which of the following conclusions can be made based on the paragraph?
(A) The students are more interesting than the teacher.
(B) The students disrespect the teacher because of her age.
(C) The students listen to more music than the teacher does.
(D) The teacher is not up to date on pop culture.
(E) The teacher is at least three times as old as her students.

DAILY SPARK ENGLISH TEST PREP

© 2004 SparkNotes LLC

Improving Sentences

Choose the answer that most improves the <u>underlined portion</u> of the original sentence. If the original sentence does not have an error, choose (A).

Every time Angela goes to the mall, <u>at least one hundred dollars is spent</u>.
(A) at least one hundred dollars is spent
(B) at least one hundred dollars are spent
(C) at least one hundred dollars were spent
(D) she spends at least one hundred dollars
(E) at least one hundred dollars gets spent

We <u>can't never</u> seem to guess what the weather is going to be like.
(A) can't never
(B) never can't
(C) can't ever
(D) could never
(E) couldn't ever

If there is an error, choose the <u>one underlined part</u> that must be changed to make the sentence correct. If there is no error, choose (E).

When the circus <u>comes</u> to town, we made sure we got <u>there</u> early so we <u>could</u> get seats
                        A   B   C

<u>close to the center ring</u>. <u>No error</u>.
              D   E

A <u>hungry flock</u> of seagulls <u>make</u> a trip <u>to the beach</u> <u>more aggravating</u> than pleasurable.
        A   B   C   D

<u>No error</u>.
      E

Identifying Sentence Errors

If there is an error, choose the <u>one underlined part</u> that must be changed to make the sentence correct. If there is no error, choose (E).

Very <u>few</u> of them <u>take</u> yoga <u>at the local health club</u> because the class is <u>too</u> advanced.
   A   B   C   D

<u>No error.</u>
  E

<u>For six long months</u>, the artist <u>paint</u> <u>the mural</u> <u>on the walls</u> of the museum. <u>No error</u>.
      A   B   C   D   E

© 2004 SparkNotes LLC

DAILY SPARK ENGLISH TEST PREP

Read the passage and choose the best answers to the questions that follow it.

(1) One could argue that considerable advances have been made in the area of health care. (2) These advances include better access to health care for patients, strides in medical research, and an increased numbers of physicians. (3) However, the health care industry has been criticized because of cost inflation, wastefulness in research spending, corrupt relationships with drug companies, and less personal contact between doctors and patients.

Which of the following could be used as the topic sentence for the paragraph?
(A) I consider the health care industry an interesting topic.
(B) Health care is very expensive, but it does great things for our country.
(C) There is some debate on the current state of the health care industry.
(D) Doctors should reconsider their relationships with HMOs.
(E) In the realm of health care, patients must choose between high costs and high quality.

With which of the following statements would the author of this paragraph most likely agree?
(A) The costs of health care far outweigh its benefits.
(B) The advances made in health care justify the rising costs.
(C) Doctors deserve high incomes because of the advances they have been made in health care research.
(D) The increase in the number of physicians has resulted in less doctor-patient interaction.
(E) The decrease in doctor-patient interaction has come under fire.

Improving Paragraphs

Read the passage and choose the best answers to the questions that follow it.

(1) The latest phenomenal in reality dating shows is a new show on the Snacking Network called "Fix a Plate and Win a Date." (2) On the show, the contestants, who are two single women, must prepare a special meal for a single guy. (3) The guy chooses the meal he likes best and then goes on a date with the girl who cooked that meal. (4) As a special twist, if the guy can figure out which girl cooked the dish he chose, the two contestants win a trip to a cooking academy in Greece. (5) The show operates on a relatively small budget, but the ratings are terrific.

Which of the following revisions does sentence 1 most need?
(A) Replace "is" with "are."
(B) Replace "reality dating shows" with "reality-dating-shows."
(C) Replace "phenomenal" with "phenomenon."
(D) Add a colon after "called."
(E) Add a semicolon after "called."

Which of the following sentences is the best conclusion for the paragraph?
(A) Sounds like a real promising thing.
(B) The producers may have discovered the formula for a number-one-rated show.
(C) However, the Snacking Network is still a fledgling network.
(D) Therefore, the producers hope to keep the show on air for at least three more seasons.
(E) Nevertheless, the show has no stars.

Complete the sentences by choosing the best answers.

In the children's tale, the _____'s white cape symbolizes his purity, while the _____'s black hat symbolizes his wickedness.

(A) hero . . . heroine
(B) protagonist . . . antagonist
(C) genre . . . denouement
(D) iconoclast . . . icon
(E) boor . . . defendant

Tim's acts of _____ earned him a dozen nominations for the "Citizen of the Year" award.
(A) altruism
(B) narcissism
(C) inconsideration
(D) rededication
(E) indiscretion

DAILY SPARK ENGLISH TEST PREP

Read the passage and choose the best answer to the question that follows it.

(1) School vouchers are like gift certificates the government gives families in order to help them pay for private schools. (2) For example, if Our Lady of the Hills school costs $5,000 per year, and a family has a voucher for $2,500, the family could use the voucher to pay for half of the tuition. (3) Opponents of school vouchers argue that the government should spend taxpayer money on improving public schools, not on sending students to private schools. (4) Some private schools dislike the voucher system because schools that receive government funding could be subject to government oversight of faculty requirements and curriculum decisions.

Some private schools do not participate in the voucher system for fear that they may lose their

(A) identity
(B) inclusiveness
(C) autonomy
(D) notoriety
(E) celebrity

Complete the sentences by choosing the best answers.

The student council broke all ties to the school administration, becoming completely

_____.

(A) abstemious
(B) cantankerous
(C) autonomous
(D) anonymous
(E) oblivious

Richard, on the run from the police, mingled with a large crowd on the street and tried to look

_____.

(A) perspicacious
(B) incongruous
(C) outrageous
(D) pernicious
(E) inconspicuous

Choose the answer that most improves the <u>underlined portion</u> of the original sentence. If the original sentence does not have an error, choose (A).

The annual bingo tournament at the retirement <u>home, drew</u> dozens of spectators.

(A) home, drew
(B) home drew
(C) home—drew
(D) home; drew
(E) home did drew

Nearly all music genres, <u>such as jazz gospel rock pop country and classical</u> appeal to me.

(A) such as jazz gospel rock pop country and classical
(B) such as, jazz gospel rock pop country, and classical,
(C) such as jazz, gospel, rock, pop, country, and classical,
(D) such as jazz, gospel, rock, pop, country, and classical
(E) such as, jazz gospel rock pop country and classical

Read the passage and choose the best answers to the questions that follow it.

(1) Workers should have a say in determining their own futures. (2) Labor should play a role in the decision-making process instead of merely reacting after decisions have been made by higher-ups. (3) We must have labor representation on the board of directors if the workers' voices are to be heard. (4) As it stands now, corporate management acts with no regard for the workers' opinions, which leads to bad morale.

In sentence 2, the word "labor" means
(A) effort
(B) workers
(C) company
(D) struggle
(E) management

With which of the following statements would the author most likely agree?
(A) Workers do not need management.
(B) Workers should run the board of directors.
(C) Management should consult workers when making decisions that affect workers.
(D) Workers should consult management when making decisions that affect management.
(E) Management mistreats and abuses workers.

DAILY SPARK ENGLISH TEST PREP

Identifying Sentence Errors

If there is an error, choose the <u>one underlined part</u> that must be changed to make the sentence correct. If there is no error, choose (E).

<u>Every time I use</u> one of my new golf clubs <u>to hit</u> the golf ball, <u>they feel</u> like it was
     A   B   C

custom-made <u>to fit my swing and my stance</u>. No error.
                  D   E

Sophie always <u>aspired</u> <u>to become</u> a professional <u>writer: but</u> she <u>didn't like</u> reading,
             A   B   C   D

spelling, or English class. <u>No error.</u>
                         E

Read the passage and choose the best answers to the questions that follow it.

(1) Experts are continuously telling us that children's television viewing should be limited. (2) Statistics show that children are watching more television now than they ever are before. (3) Yet children are not demonstrably more stupid than they were a decade ago. (4) However, the experts may be at least partially wrong.

Which of the following is the best revision of sentence 2?
(A) However, statistics show that children are watching more television now than they ever was before.
(B) However, statistics show that children are watching more television now then they ever are before.
(C) Therefore, statistics show that children are watching more television now than they ever are before.
(D) However, statistics show that children are watching more television now then they ever had been watching before.
(E) However, statistics show that children are watching more television now than ever before.

In context, which revision does sentence 4 most need?
(A) Replace "may be" with "must."
(B) Replace "However" with "Therefore."
(C) Replace "However" with "Despite."
(D) Replace "However" with "To begin with."(E) Add a comma after "be."

Complete the sentences by choosing the best answers.

Von Trapp _____ along the narrow mountain trail, never moving in the same direction for more than a few yards at a time.
(A) rocketed
(B) barreled
(C) dashed
(D) meandered
(E) galloped

Vivian's excellent grades and cheerful demeanor _____ the affection of her teachers.
(A) peturbed
(B) ensured
(C) deferred
(D) endured
(E) demurred

Read the passage and choose the best answer to the question that follows it.

(1) Intellectual property is an original idea that can be attributed to a person or a company. (2) For example, let's say you develop an idea for a TV show based on a lovable character named Mugwump. (3) If you mention this idea to a television producer and, a few months later, see a TV show about a lovable character named Mugwump, you can sue the television producer for intellectual property theft.

(4) There are many gray areas in the field of intellectual property. (5) What if a person develops an idea but never makes anything of it? (6) Should there be a statute of limitations on how long an idea can be held by a single owner? (7) Suppose two people develop similar ideas at the same time—to whom does the idea belong ? (8) Because intellectual property is a relatively new legal field, there is very little case law available. (9) However, a plethora of new suits are filed every month, so the library of knowledge is growing rapidly.

Which of the following is a true statement based on the information provided in the passage?
(A) The case law in the field of intellectual property is extremely complicated and sensitive.
(B) The case law in the field of intellectual property has reached a virtual standstill because the Internet has become so popular.
(C) The body of law in the field of intellectual property is small compared with other areas of the law.
(D) The law has become muddled due to state-of-the-art technology.
(E) Intellectual property attorneys are relatively underpaid because this area of law is so new.

Sentence Completions

Complete the sentences by choosing the best answers.

For lunch, the _____ ate a large pizza, a box of cereal, a gallon of ice cream, and a bag of chips.

(A) grouch
(B) laborer
(C) malcontent
(D) deviant
(E) glutton

With growing _____, Madison peered into the blackness of the basement and took a step forward, trying to ignore her wildly beating heart.

(A) trepidation
(B) languor
(C) enthusiasm
(D) sarcasm
(E) ennui

If there is an error, choose the <u>one underlined part</u> that must be changed to make the sentence correct. If there is no error, choose (E).

<u>When I looked</u> beneath the cushions <u>on the sofa,</u> I <u>discovered</u> the remote <u>control, and two dollars</u>
  A   B   C   D

in change. <u>No error</u>.
        E

<u>In Texas,</u> the ratio of trucks to cars must be two to <u>one; Texans</u> apparently <u>haul</u> more loads
  A   B   C

and <u>drive</u> off-road more frequently than do residents of other states. <u>No error</u>.
    D   E

Improving Sentences

Choose the answer that most improves the <u>underlined portion</u> of the original sentence. If the original sentence does not have an error, choose (A).

The first computers, which <u>had been invented</u> several decades ago, were so large that they took up entire rooms.
(A) had been invented
(B) has been invented
(C) was invented
(D) were invented
(E) can be invented

Spiders, scorpions, and centipedes don't bother her at all, but <u>snakes are the kind of reptiles that drives</u> her crazy.
(A) snakes is the kind of reptiles that drives
(B) snakes are the kinds of reptiles that drives
(C) snakes is the kind of reptiles that drive
(D) snakes are the kind of reptiles that drive
(E) a snake is the kind of reptiles that drive

Read the passage and choose the best answers to the questions that follow it.

(1) Normally, body temperature is at it's lowest, about 96.5 degrees, in the middle of the night, and rises slowly over the day until it peaks in the evening at about 99 degrees. (2) It is subject to greater variation in children than in adults. (3) More research is needed to fully understand the role of fever in controlling illness. (4) For now, it is comforting to know that a fever is usually a sign of the body working its way back to health.

Which of the following revisions does sentence 1 most need?
(A) Replace the comma after "degrees" with a semicolon.
(B) Replace the comma after "night" with a semicolon.
(C) Replace "96.5" with "ninety-six-point-five."
(D) Remove "is."
(E) Replace "it's" with "its."

Which of the following revisions does sentence 2 most need?
(A) Replace "It" with "Body temperature."
(B) Replace "than" with "then."
(C) Replace "greater variation" with "a greater degree of variation."
(D) Add "body temperature" after "than."
(E) Replace "subject to greater" with "greater to subject."

Complete the sentences by choosing the best answers.

Ossie was an _____ lawyer; his far-fetched explanations for his clients' behavior never sounded _____ to juries.

(A) inept . . . plausible
(B) skilled . . . credible
(C) unrefined . . . incomplete
(D) rehearsed . . . planned
(E) accomplished . . . polished

Trying to maintain her _____ in the face of an irate customer, Jean took a deep breath and silently counted to ten.

(A) aggravation
(B) cynicism
(C) equanimity
(D) reputation
(E) impartiality

Read the passage and choose the best answers to the questions that follow it.

(1) The Introduction to Ethics course, taught by Dr. Modesto, is always a popular class. (2) Dr. Modesto surprises her students in different ways each semester. (3) This year, on the first day of class, she explained the grading policy and the testing procedure, assigned reading, and told the class they'd be tested on the reading next week. (4) After Dr. Modesto left the room, one of the students discovered a copy of the first test on the lectern. What the student didn't know was that Dr. Modesto had put the test there herself. (5) Dr. Modesto always puts her students in situations in which they must consult their ethics in order to make a decision. (6) In this case, the students had to choose between looking at the test questions and returning the test to the professor.

Which of the following can be inferred from the passage?

(A) Dr. Modesto has a way of coercing students into doing what she wants them to do.

(B) Dr. Modesto requires the students to sign an oath of silence.

(C) Few students have heard about Dr. Modesto's classes before signing up for them.

(D) Dr. Modesto manages to catch her students off-guard each semester.

(E) Dr. Modesto's effective teaching inspires her students.

This passage's main purpose is to

(A) inform

(B) persuade

(C) investigate

(D) libel

(E) opine

Complete the sentences by choosing the best answers.

The interior designer suggests using _____ colors on bathroom walls.
(A) giddy
(B) vibrant
(C) exuberant
(D) gaudy
(E) palette

Rover's _____ to his master, Mr. Gonzales, was legendary; when Mr. Gonzales slipped and fell, Rover barked for three solid hours until help arrived.
(A) affectation
(B) fidelity
(C) trust
(D) solitude
(E) veracity

If there is an error, choose the <u>one underlined part</u> that must be changed to make the sentence correct. If there is no error, choose (E).

Down the street from <u>Rita's house</u> <u>stands</u> an enormous statue <u>of one</u> of the town's
              A   B   C

founding fathers <u>that is tall and granite</u>. <u>No error</u>.
                    D   E

Vintage <u>clothes, for some odd reason,</u> <u>fetch</u> higher prices now <u>then</u> they did when they
               A   B   C

<u>were first for sale</u> many years ago. <u>No error</u>.
     D   E

Reading Comprehension

Read the passage and choose the best answer to the question that follows it.

(1) Politicians are infamous for making vague promises. (2) Many claim that, if elected, they will implement radical changes. (3) The truth is that because of political pressure and the weight of tradition, politicians rarely, if ever, are able to implement the changes they promised. (4) Besides, many promises are made as part of the campaign effort to win over voters and are never meant to be kept. (5) Luckily for the politicians, no one seems to expect them to keep their promises.

The tone of this passage is best summed up as
(A) cynical
(B) optimistic
(C) favorable
(D) sanguine
(E) objective

Choose the answer that most improves the <u>underlined portion</u> of the original sentence. If the original sentence does not have an error, choose (A).

After stumbling through his job interview, Kevin <u>felt very upset and paces frantically</u> back and forth in the lobby.
(A) felt very upset and paces frantically
(B) feels very upset and paced frantically
(C) felt very upset and paced frantically
(D) felt very upset and paces frantically
(E) feels very upset and paces frantically

<u>The great condition she left the house in</u> before the realtor showed it resulted in an immediate offer.
(A) The great condition she left the house in
(B) The great condition in which she left the house
(C) The great condition she left the house
(D) The great condition that she left the house
(E) The great house in the condition in which she left it

Read the passage and choose the best answer to the question that follows it.

(1) Credit card companies get away with charging astronomical interest rates. (2) Often, college students are lured by the shopping freedom that comes with owning a credit card and then failed to see the actual cost until they see the bill. (3) For many, credit card debt quickly spirals out of control. (4) Many people find themselves struggling to pay off what was, in hindsight, an unnecessary or extravagant purchase. (5) Perhaps the credit card companies should take some responsibility and not allow young college students with little or no income to have cards with high credit limits.

Which revision does sentence 2 most need?

(A) Replace "failed" with "fails."

(B) Replace "failed" with "fail."

(C) Replace "are lured" with "were lured."

(D) Replace "until" with "when."

(E) Replace "and" with "but."

Complete the sentences by choosing the best answers.

The _____ sat alone in his small apartment, writing down the _____ his students loved so much.

(A) extrovert . . . clichés
(B) sycophant . . . utterances
(C) aristocrat . . . monologues
(D) prophet . . . history
(E) sage . . . aphorisms

Theo's friends _____ him not to move to Idaho, but his mind was made up.
(A) inveigled
(B) demanded
(C) implored
(D) wheedled
(E) pleaded

DAILY SPARK ENGLISH TEST PREP

Read the passage and choose the best answer to the question that follows it.

(1) Lightning occurs when an electrostatic charge in a cloud reaches fifty to one hundred million volts. (2) Lightning causes hundreds of millions of dollars in property damage annually, causes most forest fires, and kills between one hundred and two hundred people each year. (3) Despite the obvious risks of lightning, many people enjoy being outdoors during a lightning storm. (4) For those people, the exhilaration that comes from watching a majestic storm far outweighs the risks.

In sentence 4, the word "majestic" means
(A) royal
(B) noble
(C) effervescent
(D) magnificent
(E) dangerous

If there is an error, choose the <u>one underlined part</u> that must be changed to make the sentence correct. If there is no error, choose (E).

In the refrigerator <u>is</u> pizzas and hamburgers that <u>are</u> left over from <u>last weekend's</u> party

               A   B   C

<u>on the pier</u>. <u>No error</u>.

   D   E

The weather <u>was</u> so <u>cold,</u> that our breath <u>froze</u> as soon <u>as we exhaled</u>. <u>No error</u>.

          A   B   C   D   E

DAILY SPARK ENGLISH TEST PREP

© 2004 SparkNotes LLC

Sentence Completions

Complete the sentences by choosing the best answers.

Mr. and Mrs. Cole _____ Greg's college fund on an extravagant trip to Vegas.
(A) flattered
(B) squandered
(C) filtered
(D) generated
(E) deconstructed

The pool of _____ water was a haven for mosquitoes
(A) placid
(B) tumultuous
(C) stagnant
(D) opaque
(E) effervescent

Choose the answer that most improves the <u>underlined portion</u> of the original sentence. If the original sentence does not have an error, choose (A).

<u>With whom</u> did you ride home from school yesterday?
(A) With whom
(B) With who
(C) Who with
(D) With who all
(E) Whom with

All five thousand pieces of the <u>puzzle looks the same</u>.
(A) puzzle looks the same
(B) puzzles looks the same
(C) puzzle look the same
(D) puzzle, look the same
(E) puzzle, looks the same

Read the passage and choose the best answers to the questions that follow it.

(1) When the high school marching band went to Los Angeles for a band competition, the band director took us on one of those tours where the tour guide drives a bus past the homes of all the stars. (2) The band was driven by the tour guide all over Hollywood. (3) The houses blew us away. (4) Most of us had never saw such huge and palatial homes before. (5) After we got home from the trip, we talked more about the movie stars' homes than we did about the trophy we won at the competition.

In the context of the paragraph, which of the following is the best revision of sentence 2?
(A) All over Hollywood, the band was driven by the tour guide.
(B) By the tour guide, the band was driven all over Hollywood.
(C) The tour guide drove the band all over Hollywood.
(D) The band had been driven by the tour guide all over Hollywood.
(E) The band was being driven by the tour guide all over Hollywood.

Which of the following revisions does sentence 4 most need?
(A) Replace "had never saw" with "never seen."
(B) Remove the word "and."
(C) Add a comma after "huge."
(D) Replace "before" with "ever."
(E) Replace "saw" with "seen."

Complete the sentences by choosing the best answers.

The reporter's tendency to _____ his stories showed a _____ disregard for journalistic ethics.

(A) stymie . . . resolute
(B) embellish . . . blatant
(C) misconstrue . . . belligerent
(D) discombobulate . . . foreboding
(E) nullify . . . disenchanting

The castle's _____ interior design includes several _____ paintings depicting Prince James in battle.

(A) ostentatious . . . languid
(B) vociferous . . . muted
(C) baroque . . . florid
(D) ornate . . . lackluster
(E) monotonous . . . varied

DAILY SPARK ENGLISH TEST PREP

Reading Comprehension

Read the passage and choose the best answers to the questions that follow it.

(1) Probably in response to society's obsession with looking great and staying healthy, a strange new disorder has emerged. (2) Exercise addiction is a little-known but real threat. (3) Some of the signs of exercise addiction include the use of exercise to avoid personal problems or to escape from reality, the false belief that one is out of shape or fat, and feelings of guilt and depression about missing a day of exercise.

What is the main idea of the passage?
(A) Too much exercise is a good thing.
(B) Too much exercise can be a good thing.
(C) Exercise is not worth the risk.
(D) Too much exercise can be detrimental to one's health.
(E) You shouldn't feel guilty if you skip a day at the gym.

Exercise addiction, according to the article, can most likely be attributed to which of the following?
(A) obesity
(B) societal pressures
(C) tight clothing
(D) lack of knowledge about exercise
(E) guilt and depression

Complete the sentences by choosing the best answers.

The incense and soft guitar music gave an air of _____ to the yoga studio.
(A) tranquility
(B) uniformity
(C) disharmony
(D) religiously
(E) spontaneity

The political situation became so _____ that the United States pulled its Peace Corps volunteers from the country.
(A) vanishing
(B) vindictive
(C) vociferous
(D) voracious
(E) volatile

Reading Comprehension

Read the passage and choose the best answers to the questions that follow it.

(1) The use of email is more widespread than ever before. (2) Most people regard email as a useful and positive means of correspondence, but I've noticed that email has had a number of ill effects. (3) For one thing, the use of email has resulted in a deterioration of basic grammar. (4) Spelling, punctuation, and correct grammar are not highly prized or even required in emails. (5) For another thing, the prevalence of emailing has led to a breakdown in writing etiquette. (6) People no longer toil over introductions, salutations, and fond farewells.

Which of the following is the main idea of the passage?
(A) Email has revolutionized the art of letter-writing.
(B) The art of writing letters has merged seamlessly with the art of writing emails.
(C) The use of email is leading to the demise of grammar and letter-writing skills.
(D) Readers of emails are losing the ability to distinguish between proper and improper grammar.
(E) Email software should automatically check spelling.

Which of the following is true of the passage?
(A) The author is enamored of emails.
(B) The author is skeptical that email will ever catch on around the world.
(C) The author believes that email-writing is a lost art.
(D) The author disapproves of the effects of email.
(E) The author believes that emails encourage attention to detail.

Choose the answer that most improves the <u>underlined portion</u> of the original sentence. If the original sentence does not have an error, choose (A).

As the rain pounded down and the river began to flood its banks, the residents of the valley <u>packed their belongings and make their way</u> to higher ground.
(A) packed their belongings and make their way
(B) pack their belongings and make their way
(C) packed there belongings and make their way
(D) packed their belongings and made their way
(E) packed their belonging and made their ways

The photographer takes great color <u>portraits however his</u> favorite medium is black-and-white film.
(A) portraits however his
(B) portraits, however his
(C) portraits, however;
(D) portraits; however,
(E) portraits, however,

DAILY SPARK ENGLISH TEST PREP

© 2004 SparkNotes LLC

Read the passage and choose the best answers to the questions that follow it.

(1) Many popular websites allow users to download music and DVD files for free. (2) The music industry argues that music is copyrighted, and the original purchaser of a CD does not have the right to reproduce and distribute its contents. (3) According to the music industry, people who do this are breaking the law and stealing from the artists, who will never receive royalties on files that are distributed freely. (4) On the other side of the issue are the millions of computer users who download copyrighted files on a daily basis. (5) Many of them are young people who aren't aware of copyright issues. (6) Some of them are adults who blame the music industry for whatever problems it's having, pointing out that the music industry has been charging around twenty dollars for CDs that cost pennies to manufacture.

The author of the passage
(A) clearly sides with the music industry
(B) clearly sides with the file-sharers
(C) presents the issue objectively
(D) speaks judgmentally about the file-sharers
(E) speaks judgmentally about the music industry

Those in the music industry who oppose unauthorized free music downloads believe
(A) that file-sharers are basically thieves
(B) that file-sharers should get some extra leeway because they are fans
(C) that the electronic transfer of files should be made impossible
(D) that file-sharing will bankrupt artists and musicians
(E) that files should cost at least a little so that artists can recoup some of their losses

169

If there is an error, choose the <u>one underlined part</u> that must be changed to make the sentence correct. If there is no error, choose (E).

The documentary <u>highlighted</u> the many memorable episodes <u>in his career</u>, <u>including</u> not
               A   B   C

only his praiseworthy moments <u>but also</u> his moments of notoriety. <u>No error</u>.
                         D   E

Marty was so humiliated when <u>he lost</u> his contact lens at the ice skating <u>rink, and everyone</u>
                       A   B

at the rink <u>was asking</u> to stop skating until he <u>found</u> the lens. <u>No error</u>.
        C   D   E

Complete the sentences by choosing the best answers.

For a time, the identity of Mrs. Bloom's boyfriend was _____ in mystery, but then Frances spilled the beans.

(A) provoked
(B) displayed
(C) unveiled
(D) shrugged
(E) shrouded

The proctor told a joke, hoping that a little _____ might calm the students' nerves.

(A) calamity
(B) notoriety
(C) insecurity
(D) levity
(E) brevity

Choose the answer that most improves the <u>underlined portion</u> of the original sentence. If the original sentence does not have an error, choose (A).

Rodeo clowns may be even tougher than <u>the cowboys that ride the bulls that they protect</u>.
(A) the cowboys that ride the bulls that they protect
(B) the cowboys that protect the bulls that they ride
(C) the cowboys that ride and protect the bulls
(D) the bull-riding cowboys which they protect
(E) the bull-riding cowboys whom they protect

<u>After waiting in line for twenty minutes for the treadmill,</u> Boris decided to try the elliptical machine instead.
(A) After waiting in line for twenty minutes for the treadmill,
(B) After waiting in line, for twenty minutes, for the treadmill
(C) After waiting in line for twenty minutes, for the treadmill
(D) After waiting, in line for twenty minutes for the treadmill,
(E) After waiting in line for the treadmill for twenty minutes,

Read the passage and choose the best answers to the questions that follow it.

(1) The average postal carrier delivers more junk mail than first-class mail. (2) The result is a decline in postal services and an increase in costs for postal customers. (3) It costs twice as much to mail a first-class letter as it does to mail a third-class one, yet per-piece handling costs for each are the same. (4) Essentially, first-class mail subsidizes the delivery of junk mail.

The author of this passage feels which way about the effect of junk mail?
(A) despairing
(B) annoyed
(C) neutral
(D) apoplectic
(E) indifferent

In sentence 4, the term "subsidizes" means
(A) undermines
(B) cooperates with
(C) takes priority over
(D) supports financially
(E) causes

DAILY SPARK ENGLISH TEST PREP

Read the passage and choose the best answer to the question that follows it.

(1) Recent studies at a prominent research facility suggest that drinking coffee in reasonable amounts is not harmful to the heart. (2) Now coffee drinkers can relax and enjoy their morning cup of java. (3) It may be that the stress related to the concern about whether coffee is safe are actually more detrimental to one's health then actually consuming the coffee. (4) Researchers say coffee lovers should feel totally at ease while drinking their cup of joe each morning.

In the context of the paragraph, which of the following is the best revision of sentence 3?
(A) It may be that the stress related to the concern about whether coffee is safe is actually more detrimental to one's health then consuming the coffee.
(B) It may be that the stress related to the concern about whether coffee is safe is more detrimental to one is health then actually consuming the coffee.
(C) It may be that the stress, related to the concern about whether coffee is safe, is actually more detrimental to one's health, than consuming the coffee.
(D) It may be that the stress related by the concern about whether coffee is safe may actually become more detrimental to one's health then consuming the coffee.
(E) It may be that worrying about whether or not coffee is safe is actually more detrimental to one's health than consuming coffee.

174

Sentence Completions

Complete the sentences by choosing the best answers.

A wave of _____ swept over Robert when he came across the Power Rangers lunchbox he'd used in first grade.
(A) vindication
(B) misconception
(C) circumvention
(D) reprobation
(E) nostalgia

The _____ of her fans moved Ms. Starr to grateful tears.
(A) undulation
(B) adulation
(C) consecration
(D) elation
(E) procrastination

Read the passage and choose the best answers to the questions that follow it.

(1) The environmental science teacher at school has started a campuswide campaign to recycle plastics, paper, and aluminum cans. (2) She's put volunteers to work placing receptacles all over campus. (3) But her students, myself among them, have given her a hard time about the project because they do not share her enthusiasm for recycling. (4) What possible good can the efforts of a little school like ours do?

(5) Companies that recycle probably just use recycled materials to appeal to tree huggers and Greenpeace activists. (6) Besides, recycled materials are always more expensive than old-fashioned nonrecycled materials.

Which of the following is true?
(A) The author is zealous about the positive effects of recycling.
(B) The author is skeptical about the positive effects of recycling.
(C) The environmental science teacher is indifferent to the positive effects of recycling.
(D) Recycling is a moneymaking scheme devised by companies for marketing purposes.
(E) The recycling project is part of the school's curriculum.

The word "receptacles" in sentence 2 means
(A) containers
(B) recyclers
(C) classes
(D) students
(E) information centers

176

If there is an error, choose the <u>one underlined part</u> that must be changed to make the sentence correct. If there is no error, choose (E).

<u>I've narrowed</u> my college choices to <u>either State</u> <u>nor</u> <u>Tech, but</u> I still have a great deal of
   A   B   C   D

thinking to do. <u>No error</u>.
          E

The annual California Chili-Pepper-Eating <u>Contest, featuring</u> the <u>world's</u> hottest chili
                                           A   B

<u>peppers will be held</u> the third Friday in July at the <u>California State Fairgrounds</u>. <u>No error</u>.
    C   D   E

Choose the answer that most improves the <u>underlined portion</u> of the original sentence. If the original sentence does not have an error, choose (A).

<u>Fans, which attend sporting events in cold weather,</u> wear hats and coats to stay warm.
(A) Fans, which attend sporting events in cold weather,
(B) Fans, whom attend sporting events in cold weather,
(C) Fans who attend sporting events in cold weather
(D) Fans who attend sporting events in cold weather,
(E) Fans, which of whom attend sporting events in cold weather,

<u>When facing the reality</u> of unemployment, James tried to react calmly.
(A) When facing the reality
(B) When faced with the reality
(C) Whatever facing the reality
(D) Whenever facing the reality
(E) What facing the reality

DAILY SPARK ENGLISH TEST PREP

Sentence Completions

Complete the sentences by choosing the best answers.

Mark's _____ betrayals at work were in complete contrast to the _____ that characterized his private life.

(A) insidious . . . evil
(B) perfidious . . . fidelity
(C) perfunctory . . . loyalty
(D) menacing . . . malice
(E) ludicrous . . . undulation

The _____ smell burned my nose and made me cough.
(A) lucid
(B) acrid
(C) acidic
(D) acrimonious
(E) archaic

Read the passage and choose the best answers to the questions that follow it.

(1) A college student majoring in literature and psychology conducted an experiment. (2) He wrote a number of short stories targeted for children. (3) In one of his stories, a character chopped someone up with an ax; in another, a character cooked someone in an oven; in the last, a character cut off the tails of several animals. (4) When the college student sent his stories to major publishers, they reacted with horror. (5) In the report on his findings, which also included the responses from the editors he queried, the student explained that all of the events of his stories were modeled after such classics as "Little Red Riding Hood," "Hansel and Gretel," and "Three Blind Mice."

Which of the following most likely motivated the student to conduct such a study?
(A) He wanted to win a job at a major publishing house.
(B) He wanted to investigate how cultural standards have changed.
(C) He hoped to raise awareness about violence in children's literature.
(D) He hoped to impress his professor.
(E) He wanted to expose the flaws in so-called classics.

In sentence 5, the word "queried" means
(A) investigated
(B) sent an inquiry to
(C) interrogated
(D) confronted
(E) irritated

Answers

1. **(B)** visitor's
   (E) No error

2. **(C)** cryptic
   (C) imminent

3. **(B)** The author is probably in favor of the use of hybrids.
   (D) disapprove of America's reliance on foreign oil

4. **(C)** transient
   (D) subservient

5. **(B)** moves
   (E) emperor who

6. **(B)** Delete the word "usually" from several sentences.
   (B) Replace "Therefore" with "Still."

7. **(E)** sarcastic
   (A) collaborate . . . enhance

8. **(B)** polar ice caps

9. **(A)** would be prudent to dispose
   (E) bank fell

10. **(A)** won't never do
    (D) which was

11. **(C)** One way is to research the outcomes of other similar endeavors.
    (B) Replace "Therefore" with "However."

12. **(B)** The bottled water industry has a brilliant business plan.

13. **(A)** recanted
    (B) accolades . . . humble

14. **(A)** will mail
    (D) is

15. **(B)** The library wants to buy more books.

16. **(E)** clemency
    (D) hidden . . . thorough

17. **(E)** , but her hair
    (E) A dog is man's best friend

18. **(C)** The weather is still unpredictable.

19. **(E)** anecdote . . . relevant
    (E) magnate

20. **(B)** Replace "was" with "is."

21. **(E)** No error
    (C) includes

22. **(C)** Rapid advances in computer technology make it hard to stay up-to-date.
    (A) People determined to stay up-to-date should be ready to spend quite a bit of money.

181

23. **(E)** No error
    (A) One

24. **(D)** cynical about schools' motivations for sponsoring competitive extracurricular activities
    (C) apparent

25. **(A)** on the corner with the great pastrami sandwiches
    (D) scrapes

26. **(E)** Sometimes the house gets so disorganized and messy that we
    (D) not only in the United States but also in Japan

27. **(C)** Technology improved, and a steam-powered device to drive spikes was invented.
    (A) Replace "wins" with "won."

28. **(D)** enlighten . . . doctrine
    (C) prudent

29. **(B)** can overcome flawed scripts
    (D) lack the business sense to comprehend the actors' true value

30. **(A)** Me and her
    (E) no error

31. **(D)** arid . . . deluge
    (D) largess

32. **(E)** Determined
    (E) were once regular people

33. **(A)** The author likes soccer.
    (B) Soccer is a great sport, despite its unpopularity in America.

34. **(A)** shouldn't never
    (B) had got

35. **(D)** chased
    (E) music and actors'

36. **(B)** The cost of a college education is unreasonable.
    (B) unworkable

37. **(E)** neither in the Caribbean nor in the Mediterranean
    (D) told the class that there is no such thing

38. **(E)** pragmatic . . . skeptic
    (E) virtuoso

39. **(C)** TV writers and producers sometimes succeed in persuading celebrities to appear on shows.
    (E) Certain scenarios and storylines are used in many kinds of shows.

40. **(A)** because
    (A) Its

41. (D) The colleges hired extra security for the football game.
(B) nails, which had just been painted a beautiful shade of cherry red, trying to open the can of soda

42. (D) Points can even be used to go on a vacation to the Bahamas, the Caribbean, or Florida
(B) Remove the semicolon between "more" and "but."

43. (A) offer the program as a model for other interested administrators
(E) a teacher's expertise in cross-curricular subjects

44. (B) compliments . . . motivated
(E) evangelist . . . disregarded

45. (B) needs
(C) they're

46. (C) Inmates who receive vocational training are less likely to commit crimes upon their release.
(D) imprisoning

47. (C) Frank's first move was to hire a crew consisting of a carpenter, a plumber, an electrician, and a concrete expert.

48. (E) have to be
(B) nurses who work in emergency rooms

49. (B) Replace "day-to-day" with "daily."
(B) Add between sentence 1 and sentence 2

50. (D) fulfilled . . . betrayed
(B) emulate

51. (C) People have made fun of the author for his interest in infomercials.
(D) candid

52. (B) After World War II, several nations joined forces and created the United Nations.
(B) Replace "Probably" with "Unfortunately."

53. (C) had lost
(B) saw

54. (D) and lectured them
(B) night playing

55. (E) Insurance companies' business practices are unscrupulous.
(A) swindle

56. (C) Franklin believed the turkey was a powerful bird that represented America well.

(D) Replace "his" with "Franklin's."

57. **(D)** suppress . . . deployed
    (C) resilient

58. **(D)** Money spent on space exploration would be better spent on other projects.
    (A) advocates

59. **(B)** provocative
    (C) assuage

60. **(C)** Soap operas, which
    (B) Clothes from the seventies seem

61. **(D)** the author believes strongly in the necessity of research on lab animals.
    (A) the inhibition of progress

62. **(E)** His memories of riding trains have inspired my grandfather to collect trains and train memora-

bilia.
    (C) He is even thinking about opening a railroad museum here in town.

63. **(C)** reveler . . . sour
    (C) stealthy . . . elusive

64. **(B)** An increase in rain may cause a decrease in water consumption.
    (C) per person

65. **(C)** require their
    (A) neither the coffee nor the hot cocoa

66. **(B)** they
    (B) he and she

67. **(B)** than she
    (D) is

68. **(E)** Families paying off car loans and home mortgages often abuse their credit cards.
    (D) The author does not

think highly of the economists' paper.

69. **(C)** Replace "researchers" with "researchers'."

70. **(A)** prodigal . . . enthusiasm
    (A) extricated

71. **(E)** good preparation for standardized tests
    (D) enthusiasm

72. **(D)** never can find
    (C) instructions for the fire drill: quietly exit the classroom, move down the stairs, and congregate near the back of the parking lot

73. **(A)** Its
    (C) celebrities they

74. **(E)** canyon, which is over a mile deep, winds a dusty path
    (E) features

184

75. (D) a potato plant

76. (B) threw
(A) ask

77. (C) arrogant
(D) The instructor didn't feel like teaching these students.

78. (A) Perhaps if portable breath tests were made readily available, more people would become aware of their own alcohol tolerance level.

79. (A) begin
(A) hovers

80. (C) The exact location of the Ark has yet to be determined.
(D) items of religious significance

81. (C) lethargic . . . obstinate
(A) philanthropist . . . inheritance

82. (A) they
(D) the wisher

83. (E) revenue generated by the programs
(B) partial to music programs

84. (B) aesthetic
(E) lackadaisical . . . fastidious

85. (E) No error.
(E) No error.

86. (D) assure them that monsters do not exist
(E) lessening

87. (D) at that
(E) No error.

88. (A) an instructor who has
(D) they also can be

89. (E) Combine sentence 2 with sentence 3
(B) Replace "had" with "has."

90. (C) Students are no longer required to attend class in order to pass a course.
(E) Students have not been particularly angered by stringent attendance requirements.

91. (B) retires
(B) have gone

92. (C) battle
(B) a rhythm

93. (A) If infants are washed more frequently, their skin can get dried out and chapped.
(B) Regardless of these competing theories, everyone agrees that babies

don't like getting water in their eyes.

94. **(A)** intrepid
(A) fortress . . . impervious

95. **(A)** Even though running TV ads is expensive, most food companies argue that it's money well spent.
(B) Food companies prefer advertising on TV to advertising on radio.

96. **(D)** Kneepads, elbow pads, and a helmet are required
(C) have declared

97. **(D)** and features disco music
(B) goes

98. **(D)** Although experts recommend a particular study environment, students often have their own study habits.

99. **(C)** and my car gets dirty all over again
(E) the sailors filed off the ship one by one and began to search for their families

100. **(D)** Replace "besides" with "to."

101. **(D)** that role models may be more important in the development of children than lessons learned from books

102. **(D)** items,
(C) had happened

103. **(B)** lethargic
(E) curtail

104. **(E)** add to
(D) Becky made back all the money she invested.

105. **(D)** I
(B) looking

106. **(E)** Thousands of interested citizens read the feature story.
(A) room and

107. **(B)** a speech given when being sworn in
(C) the Civil War

108. **(D)** They maintain that consumers will greatly reduce the number of purchases made online if taxes are imposed. Politicians who support online taxes argue that the sales of items online will not be affected.

109. **(B)** incorrigible . . . transformed
(B) insatiable

110. **(B)** reduced stress for employees

111. **(D)** but plus
(A) hire

112. **(B)** maverick
     (E) anonymous

113. **(C)** of dirty socks, shoes, shirts, shorts, sweatpants, and practice jerseys
     (E) the sirens were very loud

114. **(D)** the media is inconsistent in its treatment of people who get arrested.
     (D) uproar

115. **(D)** Perhaps boys like the idea of wearing big rubber boots and a fire hat.

116. **(B)** Without the work of archaeologists, we wouldn't know as much as we do about ancient life in North America
     (A) Information provided by archaeologists is vital

to understanding ancient life in North America

117. **(B)** Myths that seem odd to us often make sense within the context of the culture that created them.
     (E) bewildered

118. **(C)** wouldn't never
     (D) to which nights

119. **(B)** stratum
     (D) sympathetic

120. **(E)** researchers who study all aspects of human behavior
     (B) sodas; however, most diet sodas

121. **(D)** Music videos have reduced the ability of today's teens to interpret songs for themselves.

122. **(C)** Marvin escaped without bodily harm, but he has no desire to ever get back on a bike.
     (E) Replace "different" with "differently."

123. **(C)** zenith . . . resign
     (D) enumerate

124. **(B)** The first paragraph is pessimistic, and the second paragraph is optimistic.
     (A) book

125. **(B)** tournament one
     (D) which is approximately

126. **(C)** commercials; therefore, advertisers
     (C) is the best way

127. **(C)** The residents of Pleasant Valley are of a low socioeconomic status.

(B) has not offered a response

128. **(B)** at the dogs
(C) mountains, which were very tall

129. **(D)** Replace "its" with "their."
(B) Replace "rather" with "other."

130. **(B)** it's
(B) life

131. **(A)** ambiguous . . . ambivalent
(E) trivial

132. **(C)** catastrophe
(D) The teacher is not up to date on pop culture.

133. **(D)** she spends at least one hundred dollars
(C) can't ever

134. **(A)** comes
(B) make

135. **(E)** No error.
(B) paint

136. **(C)** There is some debate on the current state of the health care industry.
(E) The decrease in doctor-patient interaction has come under fire.

137. **(C)** Replace "phenomenal" with "phenomenon."
(D) Therefore, the producers hope to keep the show on air for at least three more seasons.

138. **(B)** protagonist . . . antagonist
(A) altruism

139. **(C)** autonomy

140. **(C)** autonomous
(E) inconspicuous

141. **(B)** home drew
(C) such as jazz, gospel, rock, pop country, and classical,

142. **(B)** workers
(C) Management should consult workers when making decisions that affect workers.

143. **(C)** they feel
(C) writer: but

144. **(E)** However, statistics show that children are watching more television now than ever before.
(B) Replace "However" with "Therefore."

145. **(D)** meandered
(B) ensured

146. **(C)** The body of law in the field of intellectual property is small compared

with other areas of the law.

147. **(E)** glutton
     (A) trepidation

148. **(D)** control, and two dollars
     (E) No error.

149. **(D)** were invented
     (D) snakes are the kind of reptiles that drive

150. **(E)** Replace "it's" with "its."
     (A) Replace "It" with "Body temperature."

151. **(A)** inept . . . plausible
     (C) equanimity

152. **(D)** Dr. Morals manages to catch her students off-guard each semester.
     (A) inform

153. **(B)** vibrant
     (B) fidelity

154. **(D)** that is tall and granite
     (C) then

155. **(A)** cynical

156. **(C)** felt very upset and paced frantically
     (B) The great condition in which she left the house

157. **(B)** Replace "failed" with "fail."

158. **(E)** sage . . . aphorisms
     (C) implored

159. **(D)** magnificent

160. **(A)** is
     (B) cold,

161. **(B)** squandered
     (C) stagnant

162. **(A)** With whom
     (C) puzzle look the same

163. **(C)** The tour guide drove the band all over Hollywood.
     (E) Replace "saw" with "seen."

164. **(B)** embellish . . . blatant
     (C) baroque . . . florid

165. **(D)** Too much exercise can be detrimental to one's health.
     (B) societal pressures

166. **(A)** tranquility
     (E) volatile

167. **(C)** The use of email is leading to the demise of grammar and letter-writing skills.
     (D) The author disapproves of the effects of email.

168. **(D)** packed their belongings and made their way
     (D) portraits; however,

169. **(C)** presents the issue
objectively
(A) that file-sharers are
basically thieves

170. **(E)** No error.
(C) was asking

171. **(E)** shrouded
(D) levity

172. **(E)** the bull-riding cowboys whom they protect.
(A) After waiting in line
for twenty minutes for the
treadmill,

173. **(B)** annoyed
(D) supports financially

174. **(E)** It may be that worrying about whether or not
coffee is safe is actually
more detrimental to one's
health than consuming
coffee.

175. **(E)** nostalgia
(B) adulation

176. **(B)** The author is skeptical
about the positive effects
of recycling.
(A) containers

177. **(C)** nor
(C) peppers will be held

178. **(C)** Fans who attend sporting events in cold weather
(B) When faced with the
reality

179. **(B)** perfidious . . . fidelity
(B) acrid

180. **(B)** He wanted to investigate how cultural stan-
dards of what is decent
and acceptable have
changed over time.
(B) sent an inquiry to